Essential
Malta and
Gozo

by

CAROLE CHESTER

Carole Chester has written over 30
travel books and contributes regularly to
several publications.
She trained in journalism on Fleet Street, and
lived and worked for several years in the US.

AA

Produced by AA Publishing

Written by Carole Chester
Peace and Quiet section
by Paul Sterry
Series Adviser: Ingrid Morgan
Series Controller: Nia Williams
Copy Editors: Nia Williams,
Tony Evans

Edited, designed and produced by
AA Publishing. Maps © The
Automobile Association 1992.

Distributed in the United Kingdom
by the Publishing Division of The
Automobile Association, Fanum
House, Basingstoke, Hampshire,
RG21 2EA

The contents of this publication are
believed correct at the time of
printing. Nevertheless, the
publishers cannot accept
responsibility for errors or
omissions, nor for changes in details
given. We have tried to ensure
accuracy in this guide, but things do
change and we would be grateful if
readers could advise us of any
inaccuracies they may encounter.

A CIP catalogue record for this book
is available from the British Library.

ISBN 0 7495 0312 2

Published by The Automobile
Association

Typesetting: Microset Graphics Ltd,
Basingstoke
Colour separation: BTB Colour
Reproduction, Whitchurch,
Hampshire
Printed in Italy by Printers S.R.L.,
Trento

Front cover picture: Marsaxlokk

INTRODUCTION	4
BACKGROUND	7
MALTA	25
NORTHEAST AND EAST MALTA	45
NORTH AND NORTHWEST MALTA	52
CENTRAL MALTA	55
WESTERN MALTA	59
SOUTHERN MALTA	65
GOZO	70
COMINO	80
PEACE AND QUIET Wildlife and Countryside on Malta and Gozo	81
FOOD AND DRINK	87
SHOPPING	92
ACCOMMODATION	94
NIGHTLIFE AND ENTERTAINMENT	98
WEATHER AND WHEN TO GO	99
HOW TO BE A LOCAL	100
CHILDREN	102
TIGHT BUDGET	103
SPECIAL EVENTS AND FESTIVALS	104
SPORT	106
DIRECTORY	113
LANGUAGE	125
INDEX	126

This book employs a simple rating system to help choose which places to visit:

◆◆◆ do not miss

◆◆ see if you can

◆ worth seeing if you have time

INTRODUCTION

Malta does not flaunt its charms. This is a rocky, barren island, with no mountains and no rivers, but for those who are willing to take a closer look it has a special beauty. Doorways open on to secret courtyards, where orange and lemon trees grow, or gardens scented by wild flowers; ornate palaces hide behind plain façades. Capers and cumin grow in dishevelled abundance on the roadside, and legend and history permeate the air.

Malta is the largest of a group of five islands set between Africa and Europe at the crossroads of the Mediterranean. A four-mile (6km) sea channel separates Malta from Gozo, its smaller, greener sister, and tiny Comino has few residents and just one hotel. The other two

Living history – the tradition of painting an eye on the prow of a boat predates Christianity

islands which make up the archipelago are uninhabited. Most of the 350,000 people who live on the Maltese Islands are concentrated in about a dozen towns, mainly on Malta itself. The main island is compact – only 95 square miles (246 sq km) – so getting around by hired car or local transport is easy, and sightseeing needn't be hot and tiring. There is certainly enough to see. Malta has a long history of invasion, each wave of new arrivals leaving its own influence. Since the earliest inhabitants arrived from Sicily, the island has passed into the hands of Phoenicians, Carthaginians, Romans, Arabs, the crusading Knights of the Order of St John, Napoleon's French troops and the British. Our knowledge of prehistoric settlers relies heavily on the excavation of prehistoric sites which are liberally scattered throughout the islands; and centuries of conquest and adaptation are reflected in Malta's art and architecture, language and traditions.

Despite its small size, Malta can offer dramatic scenery, blessed with sunshine throughout the year. To the southwest, limestone cliffs drop sheer to the sea; to the east and north, gentle slopes lead to sheltered bays, coves and creeks, where colourful fishing boats are moored. There are terraced hillsides, green with vineyards; and, around the coast, forts and towers, many of which were built to repulse Turkish invasions in the 17th century.

Malta is no Monte Carlo; if you're looking for glamour and sophistication this is not the place for you. The building and tourism boom has not, so far, robbed the island of its character. Sit by any of the harbours at an open air café; charter a boat and head for the open sea; or join in a local *festa*, and you will understand why it is that visitors return time and time again. For those with imagination, and who are willing to explore, this little group of islands has an incomparable magic.

Għajn Tuffieħa Bay exemplifies the rugged beauty of the coast line

Hagar Qim gets its name from the standing stones which are the centre-piece of this megalithic temple

BACKGROUND

Malta's name may be derived from the Phoenician word for refuge, and the safe harbours of these islands, along with their strategic position at the centre of the Mediterranean, have led to a long history of invasion, siege and conquest. To understand Malta is to understand this history, for what you see today is the accumulation of past cultures.

Prehistory

Prehistoric sites are arguably Malta's biggest attraction, so it is worthwhile to learn something of their origins. Since Malta is separated from Sicily by a mere 60 miles (96km), it seems likely that early settlers made the crossing by boat in search of virgin, fertile land. Pottery dating from these times (5000 – 4100BC), decorated with elaborate patterns, has been found at Għar

Dalam. Those early colonisers would have
benefited from Malta's multitude of natural
caves, ideal for protective dwellings, but the
settlers soon developed agricultural
communities, producing wheat and barley and
living in villages (evidence of huts has been
discovered at Skorba, just outside Żebbieħ);
their religion was probably centred around a
goddess of fertility.

A new way of life seems to have emerged after
3750BC, and the next century and a half has
come to be known as the Copper Age, although
there's no evidence that copper was widely
used. During this period, the practice began of
constructing tombs for collective burial. Human
and animal bones, pieces of pottery, ornaments
and tools were found in five rock-cut tombs
near Żebbuġ, and several other examples have
been excavated, including the elaborate Hal
Saflieni Hypogeum, a complex of decorated
halls and smaller burial places. The Hypogeum
illustrates the close links – still not fully
understood – between tombs and temples. Why
there were so many temples in Malta, nobody
knows; nor why temple-building declined and
then ceased around 2500BC. The fact that
temples were extended, altered and rebuilt
over the years makes it all the more difficult to
discover their precise functions. Perhaps the
greatest era of construction is represented by
the huge Ġgantija monument near Xagħra in
Gozo; the final phase in the development of
megalithic monuments is best seen at the
cliff-top Mnajdra temples, overlooking the sea,
and the four-temple complex at Tarxien.
Towards the end of the Copper Age, settlers
turned temples into cemeteries, where they
cremated their dead and buried the ashes in
jars under dolmens. (The dolmen was a large
capstone supported by two upright boulders,
under which a chamber was dug. There are
some 20 of them scattered throughout Malta
and Gozo.) This society, now known as the
Tarxien Cemetery People, remained here for
several hundred years.

Another wave of immigrants arrived around
1450BC, establishing a beach-head at Borġ
in-Nadur, near St George's Bay. There are
about eight settlements belonging to this

period, known as the Bronze Age, including some in Gozo at In-Nuffara, not far from Ġgantija. A different group of people, called the Baħrija, settled in the southwest of Malta in about 900BC, producing textiles and fine decorated pottery. Changes in style and decoration of pottery have been vital clues to the development and decline of early civilizations. In fact, the Borġ in-Nadur and Baħrija pottery fashions overlap, and the two cultures probably existed side by side in the late Bronze Age. The strange 'cart tracks' which are found in Malta probably date from the Borġ in-Nadur period. These parallel grooves, cut into the rock, sometimes cover quite long

An ancient stone seat in the Tarxien temple complex

distances, and have perplexed archaeologists. It is thought that they mark the routes of 'slide cars', two parallel stone shafts supporting a platform, used to transport soil and seaweed.

From Phoenicians to Romans

With the arrival of the Phoenicians from what is now the Lebanon and coastal Syria, Malta enters recorded history for the first time. These new settlers came in purple-sailed boats to find refuge and shelter on their East-West trading routes. They boosted the textile industry, bringing considerable prosperity to the islands. Only when the Phoenicians were defeated at Tyre in about 600BC did their influence fade and that of the Carthaginians take over. For the next 300 years the Maltese were part of the Punic Empire, and Carthaginian temples were raised – one, on the hill of Tas Silġ near Marsaxlokk, built on a Copper Age temple site. In the 3rd century BC the Punic Wars erupted between Rome and Carthage. Malta was tossed back and forth between the two powers until 218BC, when Titus Sempronius led a successful Roman invasion. Malta became part of the province of Sicily, and gradually the islands were 'Romanised', adopting the new rulers'

The elegant stone edifice of the Roman villa and museum in Rabat

Intricate Roman mosaics at Rabat

laws and customs. The Romans further developed Malta's port areas, which led to the expansion of trade, especially in textiles (Malta's sailcloth and linens were by this time famous) and for honey. Some believe that Malta's name comes not from the Phoenicians but from the Greek word for honey – *meli*. Irrigation methods improved, increasing the wheat and olive production, and the Roman remains to be seen today attest to a progressive and prosperous society. The vast round towers dotted around the coast of Malta are thought to have been built during the last years of the Punic Wars, before peace and stability took hold.

The most notable event of these times was the shipwreck of St Paul in AD60. St Paul and St Luke were travelling from Caesarea to Rome as prisoners when their ship struck one of the rocky islands at the entry to what is now St Paul's Bay (an event recounted in the Bible, in the Acts of the Apostles). St Paul was welcomed by Malta's leading citizen, Publius, before, it is said, living in a Rabat grotto. He preached zealously, sowing the first seeds of Christianity on the island during his three-month stay. Today's tourists can visit the grotto in Rabat and see the large complex of Christian tombs known as St Paul's and St Agatha's Catacombs.

Evidence of Malta's history between the fall of Rome and the advent of Islam is scarce. No doubt the island became a strong naval base in the Byzantine era, and the Roman look-out towers may well have been reactivated and extended. By the time of Arabian expansion in the 7th century Malta would have been well fortified and garrisoned; but not well enough. After fierce resistance, the Maltese were conquered by Arab forces in AD870.

Aħrax Point
Armier Bay
White Tower
Marfa Point
Čirkewwa (Paradise Bay)
Daħlet ix-Xilep
Marfa Ridge
Melleħa Bay
Qammieħ Point
Biskra
Mistah
St. Paul's Statue
St. Paul's Islands
Anchor Bay
Popeye Village
Mellieħa
Selmun Palace
Qawra Tower
Qawra Point
Mellieħa Ridge
Xemxija
Mistra Bay
St. Paul's Bay
Buġibba
Qawra
Salina Bay
Ras il-Waħx
Wignacourt Tower
St. Paul's Bay (San Pawl il-Baħar)
Salt Pans
Ghallis Tower
Manikata
Pwales Valley
Għajn Rasul (Apostle's Fountain)
Bur Marrad
Wied il-Għasel
Golden Bay
Għajn Tuffieħa
Għajn Tuffieħa Bay
Ġnejna Bay
Roman Baths
Mġarr
Żebbiegħ
Victoria Lines
Ras ir-Raħeb
Ta' Ħaġrat Temples
Ta'l Abatija
Mosta Church Dome
Naxxar
Binġemma Fort
Mosta
Għemieri Palace
Qlejgħa Valley
Lija
National Stadium
San Anton Palace & Gardens
Attard
Rdum tal-Vigarju
Ta' Qali Craft Centre
▲212m
Mdina
Rabat
Żebbuġ
Wied Liemu
Dingli
Verdala Palace
Siġġiewi
Rdum Dun Nazju
Madalena Chapel
Buskett Gardens
Dingli Cliffs
Inquisitor's Summer Palace
▲253 m
Ġebel Ċantar
Għar Lapsi
Ħaġar Qim
Mnajdra Temples

0   1   2   3   4 km
0   1   2 miles

MALTA

Orejten Point

Bahar ic-Caghaq

Ras L-Irqieqa

St. Andrew's

Dragonara Point

Gharghur

St. Julian's

St. Julian's Bay

Gzira   Sliema

San Gwann

Dragutt Point

Balzan

Birkirkara

Ta'Xbiex

Marsamxett Harbour

Valletta

Ricasoli Fort

Wignacourt Aqueduct

Msida

Floriana

Kalkara

Santa Venera   Casa Leoni

Grand Harbour

Vittoriosa

Wied is-Sewda

Hamrun

Senglea

Xghajra

Qormi

Marsa

Paola

Cospicua

Zabbar

Wied Qirda

Marsa Sports Club

Wied il-Kbir

Hal Saflieni Hypogeum

Tarxien Temples

Museum of Religious Art

Zonqor Point

Wied Hanzir

Tarxien

Marsaskala Bay

Luqa

Il-Gzira

Marsaskala

Luqa Airport

Zejtun

St. Thomas Bay

Misrah Strejnu

Mqabba

Gudja

Ghaxaq

Tal-Mentna Catacombs

Kirkop

Marsaxlokk

Tas Silg

Orendi

Safi

Ghar-Dalam Cave & Museum

Il Maqluba

Zurrieq

Borg in-Nadur

Peter's Pool

Nigret

Birzebbuga

St. George's Bay

Bubaqra

Pinto Battery

Fort Delimara

Blue Grotto

Pretty Bay

Marsaxlokk Bay

Delimara Point

Kalafrana

Benghisa Point

Ghar Hasan Cave

Fort Benghisa

Arabians and Knights

By the 9th century the Arabs had conquered
most of the Mediterranean in the name of the
prophet Muhammed. They ruled for two
centuries in Malta, leaving an indelible
influence, most apparent in the language
spoken today, and fortified the city of Mdina
with bastions that even now separate it from
Rabat. (Mdina may first have been fortified by
the Byzantines.) They were the first to cultivate
cotton and introduce citrus fruits, which were to
become Malta's economic mainstay. Even when
the Arabs were forced to capitulate to the
Normans in 1091, they didn't disappear from the
islands; only in 1224 were they finally expelled.
Count Roger of Normandy, who led the 11th-
century Norman invasion, really only wanted to
strengthen and consolidate his gains in Sicily,
and Malta now became part of the Sicilian
Kingdom, before passing into the hands of the
Swabians, then the French, and then the
Aragonese in 1282, and eventually the Spanish
Crown. Malta was now a political pawn, its
profits exploited by one nobleman after
another, and time after time the local councils,
or *Universitàtes*, petitioned for direct rule by
the King of Sicily and a reduction of crippling
taxes. Eventually, in 1428 (with a touch of
bribery), the Maltese managed to persuade
King Alfonso V of Spain to ratify their rights
under the Crown in a Royal Charter. That did
nothing to stop repeated raids on the islands by
Berbers, Turks and Saracens, and the Maltese
took to piracy (as they had done under the
Arabs) with renewed vigour.

The Knights of St John

In 1530 Malta was given by Emperor Charles V
to the Knights of the Order of St John, in return
for the annual presentation of a Maltese falcon
to his Sicilian viceroy. They remained until the
very end of the 18th century. Originally, the
Knights were monks, known as the Hospitallers
of St John of Jerusalem, who maintained a hostel
and hospital for pilgrims in Jerusalem during
the 11th century. Wealthy Christians who
survived the First Crusade, which ended in
1099, endowed the Order handsomely –
enough to establish more hostels along

A crusading order: the Knights of St John campaigned with sword and cross

pilgrimage routes. During the fierce wars between Christians and Muslims, protection became as important as nursing, and the Order formed a military arm which was eventually to take precedence. By the 12th century, only noblemen were admitted to the Order, which was headed by a Grand Master, and its banner, bearing eight points of the cross in white on a black background, became a feared sight. The Order established itself on Rhodes in 1310, building a strong naval fleet, before Suleiman I descended with a Turkish force in 1522 and forced the Grand Master, Philippe Villiers de l'Isle Adam, to surrender the island.

BACKGROUND

For seven years the Knights were without a home, until Pope Clement VII suggested to Charles V that Malta would be an ideal base. Neither the islanders nor the Knights were satisfied with the arrangements at first. The Maltese considered the Knights' arrival in 1530 as a breach of promise; the Knights were not enthusiastic about finding themselves in such a poorly fortified place. But they saw the potential of Grand Harbour and made their base at Birgù. The strict hierarchy of the Order made it a formidable force. Only pure-blooded aristocrats could be admitted as Knights of Justice; Conventual Chaplains needed 'respectable' origins; and the Servants-at-Arms

A street scene in Valletta in the 19th century ...

. . . is still recognisable towards the end of the 20th century

were entrusted with military or secretarial duties. The Order was split into eight groups, based on nationality and known as *langues*. When a novice entered the Order he had to bring a dowry, and when he died his whole estate was taken over by the Knights. The Grand Master, elected for life by the Knights, was subject only to the Pope's authority, and was in charge of the Supreme Council, which comprised the heads of the *langues*, known as *piliers*, the Bishop and the Conventual Bailiffs or honorary Knights. Each *pilier* was assigned specific responsibilities: that of France, for instance, was the Grand Hospitaller; that of Auvergne the Grand Marshall (in charge of military affairs); the English *pilier* dealt with the cavalry, and the German *pilier* with fortifications.

Despite local objections this rigidly disciplined organisation established itself in Malta, and before long the Turkish threat brought Maltese and Knights together in a united defensive front.

The Great Siege

By the time of the Great Siege in 1565, Suleiman the Magnificent was regretting his leniency in allowing the Knights to leave Rhodes freely. In his determination to crush the Order, he headed for Malta with 200 vessels and nine thousand troops under the army command of Mustapha Pasha and fleet command of his son-in-law Piali Pasha, as well as the Barbary corsair, Torghoud Rais, also known as Dragut. By comparison, the Knights, under the leadership of Jean de la Valette, had few galleys and even fewer men.

The long and bloody battle lasted from May to September. The rest of Europe backed the Knights but sent little aid. However, a relief force was finally sent by the Viceroy of Sicily, and within a couple of days the Siege came to an end with the retreat of the Turks. Losses were tremendous on both sides, but the Knights emerged victorious.

Battered as the island was, now was the time to revive the project for a fortified city. European nobility sent money; the Pope sent his architect and the Grand Master's dream became the city of Valletta. It expanded rapidly, forming around the main streets: Strada San Giorgio (now Triq ir Repubblika, or Republic Street), Strade Merchanti (Triq il-Merkanti, or Merchants Street) and Strada Forni (now Triq l-Ifran, or Old Bakery Street). No longer were the Knights' dwellings isolated from other houses, as they had been in Rhodes. Fort St Elmo, guarding the entrance to Grand Harbour, was enlarged, and the Sacra Infirmeria was to become a great hospital (now the Mediterranean Conference Centre). Valletta was not only a fortress; it was also a centre for the arts and culture, whose buildings were lavishly embellished and furnished with only the very best. The Palace of the Grand Master became a treasure house of works of art, some of which are still to be seen today.

As Valletta grew in stature, however, so the Order grew more dissolute, breaking their vows of celibacy. Grand Master Jean l'Éveque de la Cassière was the first to try and curb their excesses, but the Knights rebelled and for a time the Grand Master was imprisoned in Fort

Valletta's harbour and city walls illuminated at night

St Angelo. His successor, Hughes Loubenx de Verdalle, was also a controversial figure. This vain man, made a cardinal by Pope Sixtus V, loved wealth and the trappings of power. Verdala Castle was built for him, and he entertained here on a grand scale in the late 16th century, even when the islanders were suffering a severe famine.

In the 17th century conditions improved: Malta was affluent and its population growing. Successful and enlightened Grand Masters such as Alof de Wignacourt (1601-1622), Antoine de Paule (1623-1636) and Jean-Paul de Lascaris (1636-1657) left their mark on the islands. It was de Wignacourt who built an aqueduct to carry fresh water to Valletta, and who erected many coastal fortress towers. De Paule, in order to disperse population, founded what is now called Paola and brought in Pietro Floriani to fortify Valletta's landfront (now Floriana). Lascaris fortified Cospicua and provided Valletta's wharves and warehouses; and his successor, Martin de Redin (1657-1660) built many castles and towers from money out of his own pocket. Personal funds were also used by Raymond Perellos y Roccaful to pay for the marvellous tapestries in the Cathedral and the Grand Master's Palace; and by Antoine Manuel de Vilhena to build the fort on Manoel Island. The longest serving Grand Master was Manuel Pinto de Fonseca (1741-1773), founder of Malta's university and under whose leadership Malta reached its zenith as an international trading centre. Ferdinand von Hompesch (1797-1798), the first German Grand Master, was destined to be the last. In 1798 Napoleon, then only 29, achieved what the

Turks had failed to do: he landed, took over
and ordered the Knights to leave (which they
did), scarcely firing a shot in the process. The
golden era of the Knights of St John was over.

French versus British

The French occupation lasted two years,
though Napoleon only stayed long enough to
draft new laws and loot a few palaces. The
Maltese requested British aid, and Lord Nelson,
fresh from victory at the Battle of the Nile, sent
a squadron to help the rebelling islands. By
1800 the French had been starved out, and the
1802 Treaty of Amiens proposed that Malta be
returned to the Order of the Knights. This was
fiercely opposed by the Maltese, and as the
Napoleonic Wars raged on, the British realised
the island's tremendous strategic importance as
a sea port. After gaining several successes over
the French, the British were officially granted
sovereignty of Malta in the Treaty of Paris of
1814.

The first British governor, Sir Thomas Maitland,
made efficient and effective reforms and
earned the nickname 'King Tom'. In the years
that followed Malta was developed as a naval
base and full use was made of her harbours and
defences. Fortifications were strengthened,
Bighi Naval Hospital created, and underground
grain storage rooms constructed in Floriana.
Small dockyards were enlarged, Drydock in
Galley Creek opened in 1848 and Somerset
Dock completed in 1871. In time, five dry docks

*In 1798 the French
attacked Malta and
displaced the
Knights as its rulers*

were built and harbourside facilities developed next to them. Malta became an important station for coaling ships, and, after the opening of the Suez Canal, a favoured port-of-call *en route* to the East and India. From the latter half of the 19th century, the island became a garrison as well as a naval base.

However, ill feeling was growing among the Maltese. The local nobility had been excluded from the management of Maltese affairs, and the islanders clamoured for self-government. A number of constitutions did give various degrees of autonomy, until in 1921 Malta was given responsibility for internal affairs while Britain, through its governor, retained control of foreign and Imperial matters. Controversy still raged, though, over the choice of an official language and economic and political administration, and the constitution was suspended in 1930 and again in 1933. Self-government was not restored until 1947.

World War II

Though Malta participated in World War I (and indeed was known as the Nurse of the Mediterranean for providing medical facilities), it was during World War II that the islands earned international accolades. At the start of the war in 1939 it was apparent that if Italy joined Germany, Malta would be left isolated, having to rely on Gibraltar for its supplies. The fear became reality, and Italian bombardment of 1940 was the beginning of the second Great

Gladiator aircraft poised to defend the island in 1940

Siege. The Maltese air force at the time only comprised four Gladiators, soon depleted to three, nicknamed *Faith*, *Hope* and *Charity*, but they took on the Italian Air Force for three weeks before support eventually arrived. The battle for Malta was the battle for control over the Mediterranean, and though Italian raids became less effective in the face of reinforcements, Germany, now installed in Sicily, began a new attack. In January 1941 alone, there were 57 raids on Malta. Despite a withdrawal of forces to help German troops on the Russian front, the raids began again in December, as the struggle continued to get supplies to Rommel in North Africa. During that month, Malta suffered 169 raids, but the islanders resisted against all odds. In 1942 King George VI awarded Malta the George Cross for heroism.

Independence

Britain provided Malta with £30 million for reconstruction and granted the islands self-government within the Commonwealth in 1947. A transfer of power did not take place, however, until 1964, when Malta was officially declared independent, with a defence agreement entitling British forces to remain for 10 years. In fact, the agreement was renegotiated and it was not until 1979 that the British pulled out for good.

In 1974 Malta became a democratic republic replacing the office of Governor-General with a

Presidency. From 1971 to 1987 the Malta Labour
Party governed the islands, with Dom Mintoff
serving as Prime Minister until his resignation
in 1985. The Nationalist Party won the 1987
general elections with a majority of one, and Dr
Vincent Tabone took over the premiership.
The Maltese themselves are devoutly religious
(predominantly Roman Catholic) and
cosmopolitan people, whose small islands have
played a large part in the history of the
Mediterranean. Their economy is largely
dependent on tourism, although ship-building
continues to play a significant role. When the
British shut down their naval and air base on
Malta, a major source of employment was taken
away, and the emphasis has been on
developing alternative industries such as food
production and crafts.

Afforestation and irrigation programmes have
been designed to help farmers counter the
problems of poor rainfall and soil erosion. A
great deal of effort is put into the task of
drawing foreign attention – in terms of both
business investors and visitors – to Malta's
situation and attractions. Having absorbed so
many international influences over the
centuries, the Maltese are now leaving their
own special impression on thousands of visitors
every year.

*Dr Giorgio Borg
Olivier, Prime
Minister of Malta,
receiving the
Independence
documents in 1964*

MALTA

The vast majority of the Maltese
population is concentrated on
the archipelago's largest island.
There are still large tracts of
open countryside even here,
however, as most people have
settled in the urban areas, and
particularly around the city of
Valletta, Malta's stately fortified
capital.

VALLETTA

This city of imposing architecture
is clustered on a promontory
between Marsamxett and Grand
Harbour. Before 1565 the walled
city of Mdina was Malta's capital,
but after their great Victory over
the Turks the Knights of St John
decided to create a new city
home which would stand firm
against all invasion. It was
Grand Master Jean de la Valette
who recognised the potential of
Mount Sceberras as a fortified
site, and plans were drawn up
with the help of the Pope's
architect, Francesco Laparelli,
for a grid-system city, a project
which was completed by his
assistant Gerolamo Cassar.
Valletta became an impregnable
fortress, encircled by massive
curtain walls. A zig-zag
arrangement of bastions meant
that the closer the enemy came,
the easier it was to fire on the
attackers along their flanks,
without the necessity of
increased arms or manpower.
The best way to appreciate the
fortifications is to walk along the
top of them; a complete circuit
should take about two hours.

*Stairs and balconies in Valletta's
streets*

In time, Valletta became a
centre of art and culture, as the
Knights embellished their
churches and residences with
the works of great painters and
sculptors. It is a city of rich and
ornate baroque churches, many
full of treasures, such as the
Greek Catholic Church on Triq
l-Arcisqof (Archbishop Street),
which contains a 12th-century
icon reputedly brought by the
Knights from Rhodes in the 16th
century. And it is a city of shady
squares, notably **Pjazza San
Gwann** (St John's Square),
location of the Co-Cathedral of
St John (see page 38); **Misrah
l-Assedju l-Kbir** (Great Siege
Square), with its allegorical
monument by Sciortino; and
Misrah ir Repubblika (Republic
Square), much loved by
café-goers, who relax under its
arcades.
The best way to see Valletta is
on foot or by *karozzin*
(horse-drawn cab), for much of
it is pedestrianised and parking
is a problem. As you wander the
streets, note the palaces – some
with plain façades hiding
handsome courtyards, some
with brightly painted wooden
enclosed balconies, which
enabled the women of a bygone
era to get a glimpse of the
outside world. Take time for a
glance at the **Palazzo Parisio** on
Merchants Street, where
Napoleon stayed briefly in 1798,
a sober 18th-century building
now occupied by the Ministry of
Foreign Affairs.
The main pedestrianised
thoroughfare, **Triq ir Repubblika**
(Republic Street), is lined with
shops and cafés. Together with
Triq il-Merkanti (Merchants

Street), it runs straight for just under a mile (1.6km) to Fort Elmo at the end of the peninsula. **Triq l-Ifran** (Old Bakery Street) runs parallel with both, as does **Triq id-Dejqa** (Strait Street), notorious for seedy bars and the only place where Knights were able to fight duels; and running across all these are Triq l-Arcisqof (Archbishop Street) and Triq it-Teatru il-Qadim (Old Theatre Street), where the 17th-century **Carmelite Church** still stands, although its 138-foot (42m) tower was severely damaged during World War II. The streets between Triq il-Merkanti (Merchants Street) and Triq ir Repubblika (Republic Street) are on flat ground (originally the entire city was to have been built on a levelled site, but the plan was too expensive); others have flights of steps leading down to the fortifications.

WHAT TO SEE

THE *AUBERGES*

The *auberge* was the accommodation used by the Knights of St John: rather like a present-day university college, with refectories for communal meals. When the Knights first arrived from Rhodes and settled in Vittoriosa, they established eight modest *auberges* for the eight *langues* (orders). After the new city of Valletta had been created and the Knights had moved there, the *auberges* became grander lodgings, although there were now only seven. (By this time Henry VIII had suppressed the English

langue.) All seven were designed by Gerolamo Cassar between 1571 and 1590, although later additions and alterations were made. For practical purposes, each building was near the section of the city wall which its *langue* defended. Today five remain, although only one may be entered – the Auberge de Provence – as most of the others are used by the Maltese government.

The oldest *auberge* is **Auberge d'Aragon**, built in 1571 and situated in Independence Square, opposite St Paul's Anglican Cathedral. The Knights of this *langue* were defenders of St Andrew Bastion and owned the Church of Our Lady of Pilar. The rather austere looking **Auberge d'Italie**, on Triq il-Merkanti, was originally built in 1574 but enlarged in 1683. Now used by government departments, it has in the past housed a museum and the Law Courts. Take a look at the windows: from the outside they seem to be irregular (in fact they are well placed for the rooms inside). Alongside the *auberge* sits St Catherine's Church, where members of the Italian *langue* used to worship. Designed by Gerolamo Cassar, who helped plan the city itself, the church interior is octagonal. Another governmental department occupies the tall **Auberge d'Angleterre et de Bavière** (originally known as the Palazzo Carnerio), overlooking Marsamxett Harbour. This was not one of the original seven *auberges;* after being bought by Bailiff Garner in 1784, it was

The Auberge de Castile et Léon

allocated to the newly formed Anglo-Bavarian *langue*.

The finest *auberge* of all is **Auberge de Castile et Léon**, built of ochre stone, originally to Cassar's design, but remodelled in 1744 by the Maltese architect, Dominico Cachia, for Grand Master Pinto. Its elegant symmetry has an Italianate look, while retaining the basic simplicity of Malta's architecture. For many years this was the British Army's headquarters; now it is the Prime Minister's official residence.

The **Auberge de Provence**, on Triq ir Repubblika (Republic Street), was begun in 1571. It is an impressive building, fronted by both Doric and Ionic

columns, and in the Knights' time it was an *auberge* known for luxury: the residents dined from iced dishes (the ice being brought from the Sicilian mountains) in a superbly ornate room. Today, the *auberge* houses the **National Museum of Archaeology**. A visit here gives a useful introduction to Malta's prehistoric sites; many of the items displayed were discovered in the Tarxien Temples and the Hypogeum (see **Background**). Two highlights are the small model of a sleeping woman, found on the Hypogeum underground burial site, and the gross lower half of a 'fat lady', removed from Tarxien to avoid erosion. There are displays from every prehistoric period, but those

from the Tarxien era are probably the most fascinating: weapons, carbonised seeds, and bowls and vases that have been meticulously reassembled (so many broken pieces of pottery have been found that breakage of vessels is thought to have been part of a religious ritual). Other exhibits include the skulls known as 'long-heads', believed to belong to Malta's first civilised settlers; and cases filled with Carthaginian jewellery. There is also a small pillar, or *cippus*, inscribed in both Phoenician and Greek. These were the inscriptions (along with those of the pillar's twin, now in the Louvre in Paris) which provided the key for deciphering the Phoenician language.

Valletta's daunting fortifications

◆◆
THE BASTIONS

The massive bastions which ring Valletta are among Europe's most awesome fortifications, and have changed relatively little since their construction in the 16th century. Four bastions protect the city's landfront: **St Michael**, **St John**, **St James** and **St Peter**. They are linked by curtain walls and additionally protected by a deep ditch, cut into the rock across the width of the peninsula. The **City Gate**, built in the 1960s to replace the war-damaged original, stands between St John and St James. Valletta's two shores are also heavily protected, with four bastions facing Marsamxett Harbour, and three facing Grand Harbour. Each bastion is honeycombed with tunnels and passages, and gives a vivid impression of the military strategy involved in the design. From **St Salvatore Bastion**, on the Marsamxett coast, you can see the unfinished **Manderaggio**, a little harbour dug into the rock to shelter the Knights' galleys in rough weather.

Within St John's Bastion are **Hastings Gardens**, where a monument marks the burial place of the Marquess of Hastings, who governed Malta between 1824 and 1826. From the gardens there is a wide view of Marsamxett Harbour and across to Floriana, St Publius Church and the

Independence Arena. The view also takes in Msida and Lazzaretto creeks, Manoel Island (used by the Knights as a quarantine station during outbreaks of the plague), Dragutt Point and Fort Tigné. This is a good point from which to admire the strong walls of the bastions of St Michael and St Andrew, 60 to 70 feet thick (18 to 21m), which were reinforced after the Great Siege. Behind St John's Bastion is the **Cavalier Building**, now housing the Embassy of the Knights of St John.

For a view of Grand Harbour, visit the **Lower Barracca Gardens**, which take in part of Castile Bastion and are the setting for another monument, built in the style of a Doric temple as a memorial to Sir Alexander Ball, who led a British squadron to the aid of the Maltese after the occupation by Napoleon.

◆
BIBLIOTECA (NATIONAL LIBRARY)
Queen's Square
This was the last of the many buildings associated with the Knights of St John, and dates from the 18th century. Ascend the majestic staircase to the collection of thousands upon thousands of books and priceless manuscripts, many of which relate to the Knights (the Order of St John's archives are housed here, covering its history from the 12th to the 18th centuries). Documents include the signed Papal Bull and the letter in which Henry VIII was proclaimed head of the Church

of England, and a collection of books printed before 1500. *Open:* Monday to Saturday, 08.30-13.00 hrs.

◆◆
FORT ST ELMO
This star-shaped fort at the tip of Valletta was built on the site of a watch-tower to protect the Knights living in Vittoriosa and St Angelo. During the Great Siege of 1565 this was the peninsula's only protection, and was destroyed by the Turkish fleet after holding out for over 30 days. The fort was reconstructed in 1567 and has been extended over the years. You need governmental permission to see round the whole fort, but not to enter the **War Museum**, which is housed in the Lower Fort (see **Directory**, under **Opening Times**, for opening hours). Relics on show are devoted to the two World Wars, including the Gladiator aircraft *Faith*, one of three which comprised Malta's airforce at the outbreak of World War II; and General Eisenhower's jeep, *Husky*.

◆
GESÙ
corner of Triq il-Merkanti and Triq l-Arcisqof
The church of Gesù, built between 1592 and 1600, is attached to the University of Malta, originally a Jesuit college (the Jesuits were expelled from Malta by Grand Master Pinto in the 19th century). Fine carvings and paintings decorate the interior: especially notable are the *Circumcision*, above the high altar, and Carracciolo's *Flight into Egypt*.

◆◆
GRAND HARBOUR

Malta's greatest natural asset has brought wealth, invasion and occupation; it has been a naval port, a trading port and an irresistible attraction to foreign fleets. Regular cruises round the harbour show precisely why it is such an ideal place to weigh anchor. Several fingers of land jut out into the water opposite Valletta's southern coast, forming a series of creeks, perfect for sheltering vessels. Two forts guard the entrance to the harbour: **Fort St Elmo** (see page 30) and, across the water, **Fort Ricasoli**, on Ricasoli Point. Beyond are the inlets of **Rinella** and **Kalkara**, running either side of the peninsula of Bighi, where a school is now housed in the former **Bighi Hospital**.

Surrounding the next inlet, **Dockyard Creek**, are the **Three Cities** of the Knights of St John: Vittoriosa and Senglea, each on its own promontory, and Cospicua (see page 42). **Fort St Angelo** looms over the harbour on the tip of Vittoriosa. During the 1565 siege, the Knights strung a chain from the fort to the opposite shore of **Senglea**, to keep out the Turkish fleet. An eye and an ear, carved into Senglea's vedette, keep vigil in case of enemy attack. Ship repairs are carried out in **French Creek**, beyond Senglea. After rounding **Corradino Heights**, the coastline leads into **Marsa Creek**, a commercial shipping centre, before turning back towards Valletta.

The city and harbours from the air

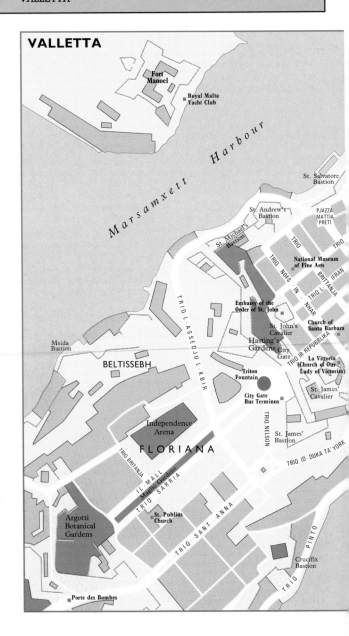

VALLETTA

Marsamxett Harbour

Fort Manoel

Royal Malta Yacht Club

St. Salvatore Bastion

St. Andrew's Bastion

PJAZZA MATTIA PRETI

St. Michael's Bastion

National Museum of Fine Arts

TRIQ NOFS IN NHAR

TRIQ BRITTANIJA

TRIQ L-IFRAN

Embassy of the Order of St. John

St. John's Cavalier

Church of Santa Barbara

Hasting's Gardens

City Gate

La Vittoria (Church of Our Lady of Victories)

TRIQ IR-REPUBBLIKA

Msida Bastion

BELTISSEBH

TRIQ L-ASSEDJU L-KBIR

Triton Fountain

St. James' Cavalier

City Gate Bus Terminus

St. James' Bastion

Independence Arena

TRIQ NELSON

FLORIANA

TRIQ ID-DUKA TA' YORK

TRIQ BRITANJA

IL-MALL

Maglio Gardens

TRIQ SARRIA

St. Publius Church

TRIQ SANT ANNA

Argotti Botanical Gardens

TRIQ PINTO

Crucifix Bastion

TRIQ

Porte des Bombes

Ball's Bastion
St. Elmo Point
St. Gregory's Bastion
Abercrombie's Bastion
St. Sebastian Bastion
Il-Fossa
National War Museum
Fort St. Elmo
TRIQ MARSAMXETT
TRIQ
SAN BASTJAN
Auberge d'Angleterre et de Bavière
Auberge d'Aragon
TRIQ L-IFRAN
St. Paul's Anglican Cathedral
Archbishop's Palace
TRIQ IT-ZEKKA
TRIQ DEJQA
TRIQ SAN
TRIQ IR
TRIQ REPUBBLIKA
L'ISPTAR
MERKANTI
St. Lazarus Bastion
Carmelite Church
Manoel Theatre
TRIQ ID
TRIQ IL QADIM
Sacra Infirmeria (Mediterranean Conference Centre)
MISRAH SAN GORG
TRIQ IZ-SANTA LUCIJA
Palace of the Grand Masters
TRIQ IL.
TRIQ SAN
Greek Catholic Church
MISRAH IR REPUBBLIKA
Palace Armoury
Church of Gesù
TRIQ KRISTOFRU
MEDITERRANEAN
MISRAH L-ASSED JU L-KBIR
Biblioteca (National Library)
TRIQ L. PAWL
TRIQ ARCISQOF
Auberge de Provence
SAN
St. John's Co-Cathedral & Museum
QADIM SAN
TRIQ IL.
Lower Barracca Gardens
PJAZZA SAN GWANN
Church of St. Paul's Shipwreck
MERKANTI
TRIQ IL- LVJANT
Fish Market
TRIQ IL GWANN
Auberge d'Italie
Palazzo Parisio
St. Catherine's Church
Victoria Gate
Auberge de Castile et Léon
Upper Barracca Gardens
VITTORIOSA (BIRGÙ)
Old Customs House
Grand Harbour
Fort St. Angelo
SENGLEA

0   100   200   300 metres

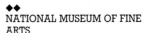

◆
LA VITTORIA
(OUR LADY OF VICTORIES)
Victory Square
Valletta's oldest church was
built in 1567 to commemorate
the victory of the Great Siege;
the foundation stone of the new
city is said to have been laid on
this site. La Vittoria was
remodelled in baroque fashion
in the 17th century, when the
façade was added. Next to the
church are the remains of one of
the city's earliest houses, and
opposite is the domed **St
Catherine's Church** (see page
26), designed by Cassar in 1576,
which contains two fine works:
Mattia Preti's altarpiece, *The
Martyrdom of St Catherine*, and,
above the altar, *Our Lady of
Sorrows*, by Benedetto Luti.

◆◆
MANOEL THEATRE
*Triq it-Teatru il-Qadim
(entrance: Triq iz-Zekka)*
This neat, oval, tiered and
gilded 18th-century theatre was
built to the order of Grand
Master Manoel de Vilhena in
1731, and is one of Europe's
oldest theatres still in use. A
bust of the Grand Master can be
seen in the foyer. The Manoel
was restored to its true
splendour in the 1960s, after a
period of neglect, and is now
Malta's national theatre, staging
opera, ballet and drama during
the October-May season. The
lush interior includes an
elaborately decorated
Presidential Box, where the
Grand Master used to sit.
Guided tours of the Manoel
Theatre take place on weekday
mornings.

◆◆
NATIONAL MUSEUM OF FINE
ARTS
Triq Nofs-in-Nhar
The white 16th-century palace
which houses this museum (the
former Admiralty House) was
used initially by the Knights of St
John. After it had been rebuilt in
1761 it was occupied by a
number of distinguished people,
including the French Admiral
Suffren and the Vicomte de
Beaujolais (Louis Philippe's
brother). From 1821 to 1961 it
was the residence of the
Commander-in-Chief of the
British Mediterranean fleet, and
near the top of the magnificent
staircase plaques list all the
Commanders-in-Chief, among
them Nelson, although he didn't
live here. The museum
surrounds a courtyard where
outdoor exhibits are displayed
in summer.
The paintings on display are
mainly 17th-, 18th- and
19th-century, and cover a
variety of European schools of
art. Of particular note is *A Man
in Armour*, by Tintoretto, and a
collection of Flemish works.
Later compositions include
those by Antoine de Favray,
Claude Joseph Vernet and Louis
de Cros, but pride of place goes
to the masterly work of Maltese
artists, including the
20th-century sculptor Antonio
Sciortino, and 17th-century
Mattia Preti.
If time is short, head first for the
basement, where items used in
the Knights' hospital may be
viewed: vases, apothecary jars
and some of the silver plates
which were used in the Sacra
Infirmeria (see page 37).

The Palace of the Grand Masters

◆◆◆
PALACE OF THE GRAND MASTERS
Triq ir Repubblika (main entrances: Triq il-Merkanti, Triq it-Teatru il-Qadim and Triq l-Arcisqof)

Today this building is the Presidential Palace, seat of the House of Representatives and headquarters for several governmental departments. It is also Valletta's most treasured museum. Originally, when it was built in 1569, this was a private timber house for the Grand Master. Later, Gerolamo Cassar was commissioned to enlarge it. The Grand Master, Head of the Sovereign Military Order of St John of Jerusalem, lived for most of the year in this building,

which was much more than a private home, as this was where rules were made and orders given.

The spacious, two-storey edifice encloses two courtyards: **Neptune Court**, named after its bronze central statue, and the inner **Prince Alfred Court**, which is slightly smaller. Before you enter the palace, look up at the Moorish clock (1745), installed by Grand Master Pinto; its mechanical Turkish figures gong the hours. The staircase up into the palace, though not open to the public, is a marvellous architectural feature in itself: you can just imagine the Knights in full armoured regalia,

climbing the low steps to meet the Grand Master.

One of the most attractive chambers is the **Tapestry Room**, or Council Chamber, where Malta's Parliament formerly met. Here you can sit and admire the famous Gobelin tapestries given to the Order by Grand Master Ramon Perellos in the early 18th century. They feature real and fanciful creatures and exotically attired Indians.

The grandest public room is the **Hall of St Michael and St George**, or Throne Room, which takes its name from the order of chivalry which had its investiture here in 1818. Under the beamed and carved ceiling is a frieze by Matteo Perez d'Alesio, one of Michelangelo's pupils, showing scenes of the Great Siege. Opposite the throne, the beautifully carved gallery was once the stern of the flagship in which Grand Master de' l'Isle Adam sailed from Rhodes to Malta. You can enter the Hall from the **Entrance Corridor** whose ceiling was painted in 1724 by Nicolo Masoni da Siena.

The **Hall of Ambassadors**, or Red Room, is hung with damask and features several interesting if rather heavy and dark portraits of notables of their time, including a de Troy study of Louis XIV, Louis XV by van Loo and Catherine II of Russia by Levitzky. Another d'Alesio frieze depicts the story of the Knights from 1309 to 1524. This is the room where foreign envoys present their Letters of Credence to the Head of State.

Vivid tapestries hang in the Palace

In the **Yellow State Room**, previously the pages' waiting room and now used for conferences, there are paintings by Batoni and Ribera, 16th-century Urbino vases and a Boulle calendar clock.

Prince Alfred's Court leads into the **Armoury**, which contains thousands of pieces of armour from all over Europe. One of the most striking items is the gold damascened ceremonial suit of armour made for Grand Master Alof de Wignacourt, and his sapping suit, weighing 110lbs (50kg). There are also captured Turkish arms, including a sword said to belong to the corsair Dragut, as well as suits of armour belonging to Grand Masters Jean de la Valette and Martin Garzes.

Opposite the palace and across the square is the **Chancery**, which once housed the Grand Masters' bodyguard.

◆◆
SACRA INFIRMERIA (GREAT HOSPITAL OF THE ORDER)

Triq l-Isptar il-Qadim

Now the home of the Mediterranean Conference Centre, the Knights' hospital was built in 1575 with a 520-foot (155m)-long Great Ward. Over a hundred tapestries once decorated this room where the sick and insane from all walks of life were treated and served food on silver dishes (now in the National Museum of Fine Arts) by the Knights themselves. In one of the halls, you can watch an hourly 45-minute audio-visual presentation entitled *The Malta Experience* (see **Children**, page 102, for details).

VALLETTA

♦♦♦
ST JOHN'S CO-CATHEDRAL
Pjazza San Gwann
After the Great Siege, Grand
Master de la Cassière was keen
to make Valletta Malta's
religious centre as soon as
possible, and in 1577 he
financed what is considered to
be Gerolamo Cassar's
masterpiece. It was built as the
conventual church of the Order,
and adorned lavishly by the
Knights (though many of the
treasures were looted by the
French in 1798). St John's is
known as a Co-Cathedral
because it shares its status –
granted in 1816 by Pope Pius
VII – with the earlier cathedral
in Mdina.

Don't be put off by the heavy,
uninspiring exterior. Inside this
centre of worship for the 'monks
in armour' is a glorious display
of baroque art. There is
scarcely a part of the church
that isn't gilded, painted or
decorated, including the
elaborately inlaid marble floor
and tombs. The 189-foot
(57m)-long, barrel vaulted nave
rises to 64 feet (19.5m); here the
17th-century Calabrian painter,
Mattia Preti, has depicted
scenes from the life of St John
the Baptist in oil-on-stone
paintings. The whole sweep of
the structure leads your eyes
automatically to the high altar,
designed in 1681 by architect
Lorenzo Gafà. Behind its
elaborate combination of silver,
marble and lapis lazuli is a
sculpture of the *Baptism of
Christ* by Giuseppe Mazzuoli. If
you ask why the altar's flanking
pillars are gold towards the top
and white towards the bottom,
you might be told that this is
because Napoleon's troops
scraped off as much gold as
they could reach; but the real
culprit was damp.

The tombs of the first 12 Grand
Masters are contained in the
crypt, including those of Villiers
de l'Isle Adam and Jean de la
Valette. The crypt may be
visited between 10.00 and 12.00
hrs upon request. In the **sacristy**
are paintings by Stefano, Pieri,
Preti and de Favray.

A door to the right of the altar
leads to the **Oratory and
Museum**. This is where the
Cathedral's greatest treasure
can be seen: Caravaggio's
enormous, dramatic painting of
The Beheading of St John.
Caravaggio was commissioned
to paint several works by the
Grand Master, and was even
received into the Order, but
after a contretemps with one of
the Knights he left Malta in
disgrace in 1608.

The museum houses ancient
silver and embroidered
vestments, but the focal items
are the superb Judocus de Vos
tapestries, made in Belgium in
the 17th century and based on
paintings by Rubens and
Poussin. During the Festival of
St John in June, these tapestries
are displayed in the nave of the
Cathedral.

Chapels line both sides of the
nave, most of which were built
by the *langues* of the Knights
and feature busts or monuments
commemorating the Grand
Masters. The **Chapel of the
Blessed Sacrament** has solid
silver gates, which, it is said,
were painted black to foil the
pillaging French in 1798.

◆
ST PAUL'S SHIPWRECK
Triq San Pawl

Apart from the Cathedral, this is perhaps Valletta's most notable church. Completed in the 16th century (the façade was a later addition), it houses a rich collection of gold and silver ornaments, but the most striking

Built for the Knights, St John's was given Cathedral status in 1816

treasure is a baroque statue of St Paul sculpted by Melchior Gafà in 1657. Other notable features include Filippo Paladino's altarpiece of St Paul's shipwreck, and the early 20th-century ceiling frescos.

◆
SANTA BARBARA
Triq ir Repubblika
Situated between Triq Nofs
in-Nhar and Triq Brittanja,
this 18th-century church was
designed by Giuseppe Bonici
and used by the Knights of
Provence. It is laid out in an
unusual oval shape and has a
gold-covered Virgin Mary on its
façade.

◆
UPPER BARRACCA GARDENS
Castile Place
This is where the Knights of St
John would stroll, gossip and, no
doubt, plot. Nowadays the
18th-century gardens, planted
on the training ground of the
Italian *langue* overlooking
Grand Harbour, are the setting
for several statues, including
Antonio Sciortino's group of
children, *Les Gavroches;* a
large monument honouring Lord
Strickland, who was Prime
Minister from 1927 to 1932; and
a bust of British Prime Minister
Sir Winston Churchill. The
somewhat plain tomb of Sir
Thomas Maitland ('King Tom'),
the Governor of Malta from 1813
to 1824, is also here.

Environs

◆
FLORIANA
This modern suburb of Valletta
was built in 1634 as an added
protection against Turkish
invasion on the city's land
approach. It was named after
the Italian military engineer,
Paolo Floriani, who was sent to
Malta by the Pope to
recommend extra defences.
Floriana therefore has its own

bastions, outside the Valletta
fortifications. In 1722 work
began on the town itself, with
gardens and spaces preventing
its encroachment on the
defences. Gardens are still a
major feature of Floriana, almost
bisecting the suburb. Stretching
from City Gate, opposite the
Phoenicia Hotel, are the **Maglio
Gardens**, which contain a statue
of *Christ the King* by Antonio
Sciortino.
This area of Floriana was first
used as an exercise ground for
Knights. The **Argotti Botanical
Gardens**, beyond the Maglio
Gardens, were planted in 1774
and have a collection of rare
plants and cacti. Below these
are the **Sa Maison Nursery** and
the **St Philip Neri Gardens**. As
you walk along the Maglio
Gardens from Valletta, the
Independence Arena spreads
out to your right, and, on the
other side, covered circular
granary pits, used by the
Knights for storage, form part of
St Publius Square. **St Publius
Church**, a twin-towered,
18th-century edifice named
after the Roman Governor of the
island, who was converted by St
Paul to become Malta's first
bishop, stands here, and,
behind it, the round 17th-
century church of **Sarria**, built
by Mattia Preti and decorated
with seven of his paintings.
Floriana's most notable
landmark is the double arched
gateway, **Porte des Bombes**,
originally a single arch built
during the Grand Mastership of
Perellos y Roccaful in the 18th
century; the other arch was
added in the 19th century, for
aesthetic balance.

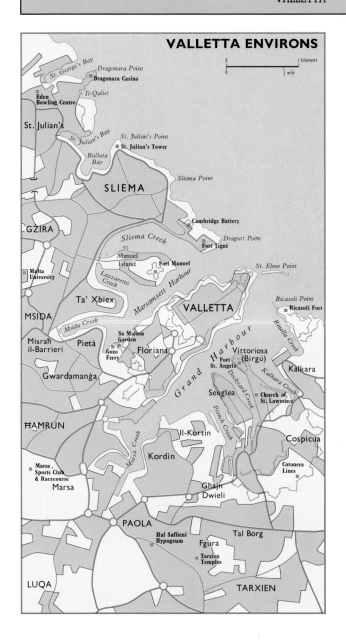

VALLETTA ENVIRONS

0 ———————————— 1 kilometre
0 ———————————— mile

St. George's Bay

Dragonara Point

■ **Dragonara Casino**

Il-Qaliet

■ **Eden Bowling Centre**

St. Julian's

St. Julian's Bay

St. Julian's Point

■ **St. Julian's Tower**

Balluta Bay

Sliema Point

SLIEMA

■ **Cambridge Battery**

GŻIRA

Sliema Creek

Dragutt Point

■ **Fort Tigné**

Manoel Island

■ **Fort Manoel**

St. Elmo Point

■ **Malta University**

Lazzaretto Creek

Marsamxett Harbour

Ta' Xbiex

VALLETTA

Ricasoli Point

■ **Ricasoli Fort**

MSIDA

Msida Creek

Rinella Creek

Misraħ il-Barrieri

Pietà

■ **Sa Maison Garden**

■ **Gozo Ferry**

Floriana

Grand Harbour

Vittoriosa (Birgù)

Fort St. Angelo

Kalkara

Kalkara Creek

Gwardamanġa

Senglea

■ Church of St. Lawrence

Dockyard Creek

French Creek

ĦAMRUN

Il-Kortin

Cospicua

Kordin

Marsa Creek

Cotonera Lines

■ **Marsa Sports Club & Racecourse**

Marsa

Għajn Dwieli

PAOLA

■ **Ħal Saflieni Hypogeum**

Tal Borg

Fgura

■ **Tarxien Temples**

LUQA

TARXIEN

◆◆◆
THE THREE CITIES

Across Grand Harbour, to the south of Valletta, are the three historic cities where the knights first settled: Vittoriosa, Senglea and Cospicua, collectively known as The Three Cities. Because they are located close to the dockyard, they were a direct target area during the last World War and suffered a great deal of damage. They can be reached by bus from City Gate or by car via Marsa, but you could also negotiate a price with local boatsmen for a trip across the harbour.

When the Knights first came here, there were three separate small towns. Now, urban growth has joined them to each other and to the Kalkara waterfront, and they have become a jumble of mellow buildings, clustered around and behind French and Dockyard Creeks.

Vittoriosa was chosen by the Knights as their first home when they arrived in Malta. The town, then known as Birgù, already had a long history and several noble buildings (which were quickly adapted to the Knights' lodging needs), and had the particular advantage of Fort St Angelo, guarding the tip of the peninsula.

The **Church of St Lawrence**, on the waterfront, is a 17th-century building on the site of the island's first parish church, later used as the Knights' conventual church and constructed in 1691 with a richly painted and marbled interior (only its dome was lost to the bombs). Inside, there is a huge statue of St Lawrence carrying the grid-iron on which he was martyred, which is taken through the streets every 10 August for the Saint's Day procession.

Stroll up Il-Majistral Street in the heart of the town, past the 1534 **Auberge d'Angleterre**, and the **house of Sir Oliver Starkey**, who resisted Henry VIII and stayed loyal to the Order, even though the English *langue* had been suppressed, to **Vittoriosa Square**, where Grand Master la Valette would review the troops, and **St Joseph's Oratory**, with its adjacent little museum.

At the top of Il-Majistral Street and bordering Vittoriosa Square are three other *auberges:* **Auberge d'Allemagne**, **Auberge de France** and **Auberge d'Auvergne et Provence**, all originally built in the 1530s. **Palazzo del Sant' Uffizio**, or the Inquisitor's Palace, stands in Triq Boffa, between Vittoriosa Square and the town's landfront fortifications. Built around the Castellania (the Knights' civil courts), it was enlarged in the 17th century. The grand, Italianate house is set around three courtyards, and provided headquarters for the Inquisition, which was established in 1562 and located away from the Order's own city of Valletta. Grand Master de la Cassière, worried that the spirit of Reformation might undermine the Knights' orthodoxy, had made the mistake of asking the Pope to lend a helping hand. The man sent as a papal delegate quickly acquired power, and his successors attained even greater influence. Although the Inquisitors were

The battlements of Vittoriosa

considered less extreme than their notorious Spanish counterparts, they were soon hated as much by the Order itself as they were by the local people. Inside the palace, the prisoners' cell leads to a Judgement Room, whose door was deliberately built low so that anyone entering would be forced to bow to the Inquisitor. The living rooms are opulent and decorated with lovely murals; one displays the coats of arms of all the Inquisitors who were stationed here, the last being Julius Carpineo, appointed in 1793. The most interesting items displayed include the Inquisitor's two-wheeled black carriage, which would be pulled through the streets by two men, and a rococo bureau which opens up into a gilt and velvet-lined altar.

Fort St Angelo's history is as old and rich as that of Malta itself. There had been a temple on the tip of the promontory since about 1500BC; Phoenicians, Greeks and Romans all worshipped here. It was the Arabs who first used the site for

defence, erecting a small castle, and when they were driven out by Roger the Norman in 1090 the first small church was built. In 1430, the castle was given to the de Nava family, who built a residential palace and the Chapel of St Anne. By this time St Angelo was a citadel, so it was a natural choice for the Knights to improve the defences sufficiently to withstand the Turkish attack later that century. When the Knights moved to Valletta in 1571, St Angelo was handed to the governor of the fort. It was restored in 1681 by the Spanish king's engineer, Don Carlos Grunenberg, but slipped into oblivion thereafter until 1902, when the wharf and lower fort were built. From 1912 the British navy used it as their Mediterranean base, until they departed from Malta; the fort is now undergoing conversion into a tourist complex.

Senglea was badly damaged during World War II and does not bear much resemblance to the 16th-century city built for the Knights and known as L'Isla. Its present name recalls Claude de la Sengle, the Grand Master

who fortified the city after the Great Siege. There is little to see now – post-war rebuilding has not been very attractive – but the **Church of Our Lady of Victory**, in the centre of the main square, is worth seeing: the original 17th-century building was destroyed in the war, and it has been reconstructed to an ornate design.

There are impressive views from the gardens at **Isola Point**, where a vigilant eye and ear are carved on the sentry post (see page 31).

Cospicua (once known as Bormla), at the head of a busy creek, also had to be rebuilt, but

A view of Senglea across the Grand Harbour from Valletta

it is still ringed by the formidable walls of the 5,000-yard (4,572m)-long **Cotonera Lines**, named after Grand Master Nicholas Cotoner, who had them constructed in the 17th century. The fortifications were never put to the test – which was just as well, as it would have been difficult to find enough men to defend the line. Before Cotoner's defences took precedence, work had already started on a circle of bastions known as the Margherita Lines: these were not completed until the mid-18th century.

NORTHEAST AND EAST MALTA

Most of Malta's population is
concentrated in the area
surrounding Valletta and its two
harbours. This is where the
Knights of St John developed
their capital and major defence
system; today it is where the
biggest resorts have sprung up,
providing a wide range of
tourist facilities.

WHAT TO SEE

◆
BIRKIRKARA

The old part of Birkirkara,
established in the 16th century,
has the look of a traditional
Maltese village, with narrow
streets and simple one-storey
houses set next to more stately
balconied mansions. New
buildings, roads and an
industrial area have now
extended the place, but it still
has a lot of character. The
parish is home to one of the
island's largest and most
beautiful churches, the
Collegiate Church of St Helen,
designed by Maltese architect
Domenico Cachia in the 18th
century: a tall, baroque church,
heavily gilded and painted
inside. Vittorio Cassar's **Church
of the Assumption** was
Birkirkara's original parish
church, built in 1617.
Bus routes from Valletta:
71, 72, 78

◆
GHARGHUR

There are wonderful views from
this medieval hilltop village on
the Naxxar Ridge. No fewer
than four 17th-century churches

are found here, dedicated to **the
Assumption**, **St Nicholas**, **St John
the Baptist** and the village's own
patron saint, **St Bartholomew**.
The latter was designed in 1628
by Tomasso Dingli, and has a
sundial on the façade – a rare
feature in Maltese churches.
The gilded interior contains a
curious statue of a saint
(beneath the altar), comprising
real bones, though not those of
the saint in question. Għargħur
marks the northern end of the
Victoria Lines, a series of
fortifications built by the British
at the end of the 19th century
along a high ridge of ground
caused by a natural fault. The
lines run across the island to
Baħrija, cutting off the northwest
corner of Malta and punctuated
with forts and excellent viewing
points.
Bus route from Valletta: 55

◆
GZIRA

Gzira is basically a residential
extension of Sliema (see page
49). There are many amenities
along its wide promenade and a
bridge links it with **Manoel
Island**, whose fort, built in the
18th century by Grand Master
Antoine Manoel de Vilhena,
now houses the Valletta Yacht
Club.
Bus routes from Valletta:
60, 61, 62

◆
ḤAMRUN

This is the industrial suburb of
Msida (see page 46), with a
busy high road and a new
student quarter on its periphery
at Blata il-Bajda. Although a
somewhat uninspiring place in
itself, this is a very good

shopping centre. As you travel through the area you will pass the **aqueduct** built in the 17th century by Grand Master Wignacourt to bring water into Valletta. **Santa Venera**, a suburb to the west, is worth a stop to see the **Casa Leoni** (House of Lions), which was built in 1730 for Grand Master de Vilhena and set in beautiful formal gardens.
Bus routes from Valletta: 71, 73.

KALKARA

This small fishing village at the entrance of Grand Harbour was almost totally rebuilt after the last World War. The creek is bounded by the bastions of Vittoriosa and St Angelo on one side, and by the Bighi headland on the other, and is the site where the *dgħajsas* (water taxis) are constructed and repaired.

Above the village, the **Royal Naval Hospital**, now a school, was used by Napoleon and by Lord Nelson; originally designed as a villa, the building was extended in the mid-19th century.
Bus route from Valletta: 4

LUQA

An important route town for Malta's airport and southern villages, Luqa had little left after World War II. The 15th-century **Church of the Assumption** did survive the bombs, however, and the other parish church of **St Andrew**, containing Mattia Preti's original 17th-century altarpiece, has since been rebuilt.
Bus route from Valletta: 36

MARSASKALA

On the southeast coast, at the head of a bay of the same name, sits this quaint fishing village, which has recently emerged as a tourist area with holiday complexes and a large first-class hotel, the Jerma Palace. Known locally as Wied il-Ghajin, the village is a pleasant spot with rocky bathing places and facilities, including the recently converted **St Thomas Bay and Tower** restaurant complex. **St Thomas Tower** was built to protect Marsaskala after a Turkish landing in 1614. Another 17th-century tower guards St Thomas Bay: **Mamo Tower**, a cruciform building with a circular room at its centre.
Bus route from Valletta: 19

MSIDA

This former fishing village, set in one of the inner creeks of Marsamxett Harbour, has grown to town scale and is now part of a ribbon development between Pietà and St Andrew's. It is a lively and colourful place, busy with boats and yachts. The most imposing structure is **St Joseph's** parish church, built in 1893; and the most interesting site is along the Birkirkara road, where a vaulted washing place stands on the source of a natural spring. It was built in the 18th century by the German Knight, von Guttenberg.
To the north, at **Tal 'Qrogg**, is Malta's University, which moved here from its Valletta buildings in the 1960s.
Bus routes from Valletta: 60, 61, 62

The Hypogeum burial site, Paola

◆◆◆
PAOLA

Some consider Paola purely as a workers' suburb of Valletta, but it should be given credit in its own right, for it has a long and distinguished history. Paola was founded in 1626 by Grand Master Antoine de Paule as a summer resort; he provided funds to build the **Palace of San Anton**, and the parish church of **St Ubaldesca**, designed by Vittorio Cassar. More prosperous times gave the town a great new church in 1924; it stands on the main square, which is the scene of an open air market.

The reason for Paola's high star rating, however, is the **Hal Safilieni Hypogeum**, which represents the quintessence of temple art. As its Greek name (*Hypogeum:* subterranean chamber) suggests, this prehistoric site is underground

and is probably the most fascinating of Malta's ancient monuments. Claustrophobics may not appreciate the vast labyrinth of caves carved from soft limestone, but it would be a pity to miss seeing such a well preserved and intriguing place. Basically, this is a catacomb with a series of rock-cut chambers at different levels, descending to a depth of 40 feet (12m), but it was used partly as a temple of worship and partly as a burial place.

The highest level is the oldest: archaeologists believe it was created around 3000BC, and was largely used for burials. The two lower levels show more sophisticated work, with elaborately carved walls, probably dating from between 2500 and 1800BC.

The middle level is the most

impressive; here you will see corbelled doors and niches resembling features of megalithic surface temples. Some rooms are decorated with spirals and hexagons, and in the **Holy of Holies** you can see traces of red ochre on some of the walls (the ritual colour of death), denoting a dual function burial place and shrine. The 'Sleeping Lady' figure now in the National Museum (see page 34) was discovered on this middle level. In the rectangular **Oracle Chamber**, deep voices will create an echo; usually only men can create the effect. At the deepest part of the complex, cubicles have been cut into the rock 36 feet (11m) below the ground. The complex covers 8,600 square feet (799 sq m) and remains found here

A colourful scene at St Julian's

suggest that the Hypogeum held as many as 7,000 bodies. Although its exact function still baffles, archaeologists believe that it was probably the most sacred site of its time.

Only about 15 visitors can enter the Hypogeum at any one time, for three quarters of an hour. In the summer visits take place Monday to Sunday at 08.30, 10.00, 11.30 and 13.00 hrs; in the winter at 08.30, 10.00, 11.30, 13.00, 14.30 and 16.00hrs Monday to Saturday and 08.30, 10.00, 11.30 and 14.00 hrs on Sunday.

Bus route from Valletta: 5

◆
QORMI

Come to this medieval town to try some tasty Maltese bread and pasta: Qormi has a long-established and lively tradition of baking, and was once known as Casal Fornaro (Village of Bakeries). There are some handsome old buildings in its narrow streets. Its church, **St George** (1584), is one of the most imposing in Malta, with its twin spires and Renaissance façade.

Bus routes from Valletta: 88, 91

◆
ST JULIAN'S

St Julian's, which has grown from a fishing village to a popular resort, has no 'sights' as such, but it is a delightful place to visit, with pretty streets and houses and two attractive bays: **Balluta** and **Spinola**. This is one of Malta's liveliest centres for cafés and nightlife, and, together with tiny **St George's Bay**, slightly further along the coast, offers accommodation,

watersport facilities and even a casino. Not surprisingly, St George's can get very crowded. **St Andrew's**, slightly inland, was once a large military base, but has also become part of the island's tourist development. All along the coast here the land slopes gently to the sea and there is plenty of rock bathing.

Bus routes from Valletta: 62, 67, 68

◆◆
SLIEMA

Malta's most modern town is a fashionable residential resort on a promontory facing Marsamxett Harbour, which has grown fast to become a popular tourist base. Its shops, hotels and restaurants include some of the best on the island. A three-mile (5km) promenade runs along the seafront, where you can take the air, catch the ferry to Gozo, or eat in a restaurant (Il-Fortizza) which is housed in a converted 19th-century fort. One of the many defences built by Grand Master de Redin stands at the other end of the promenade: **St Julian's Tower**, erected during his three-year rule in the 17th century. **Fort Tigné**, on Dragutt Point, was built in 1761 by Grand Master Pinto as the last of the defences for Valletta. It was intended as an auxiliary fort, helping Fort St Elmo guard the entrance to Marsamxett Harbour.

Sliema's two main streets are **The Strand**, along Sliema Creek, and **Tower Road**, on the peninsula's northern shore, which is good for shops, as is **Bisazza Street**.

Bus routes from Valletta: 60, 61, 62, 63, 64

Carved stone blocks at Tarxien

◆◆◆
TARXIEN

The village of Tarxien had, in effect, merged with the neighbouring town of Paola, but its name achieved historical significance with the discovery of the biggest prehistoric site on the island.

When the site was excavated between 1914 and 1919 by Sir Themistocles Zammit, remains of a temple complex were found dating from the latter half of the third millennium BC. The temples are perhaps the highest achievement of the Maltese Copper Age, and suggest a sophisticated community, whose people were skilled in building and carving without the aid of metal tools. At the entrance to the temples is a small **museum**, which houses replicas of some of the carved blocks and prize finds from the complex. (The originals are in the National Museum in Valletta, see page 28).

As you enter the first or south temple, you can see the remains of a larger than life statue, that originally stood 9 feet (3m) high; what now remains is the bottom 3 feet (1m), showing a pair of sturdy legs and a pleated skirt. Close by, blocks of stone are carved in relief with swirling patterns.

From the south temple you pass into the central temple, which is perhaps the most evocative part of the site. Walking along the paved courtyard, with its circular hearth, and admiring the relief wall carvings of bulls and a suckling sow, you can picture the ancient ceremonies which took place here and involved animal sacrifices and libation-pouring.

Two steps lead up to the eastern temple, and here, again, the stones come alive in the inner chamber, with its secret hole, through which a priestly oracle made predictions in riddles.

The people who built the Tarxien temples vanished from recorded history in around 2000BC. However, the buildings continued to be used by a new community, known as the Tarxien Cemetery People. Most of the evidence for their existence comes from this site, which was used as a place for mass cremations and had its floors levelled for that purpose. The ashes were placed in large urns, which were left on the site, and around them were placed pieces of fabric, jewellery and tools.

Another temple on the Tarxien site was built around 3000BC; all that remains of it are a few scattered stone blocks.

For opening hours see **Directory**, under **Opening Times**.

Bus routes from Valletta: 8, 11, 26

◆
ŻABBAR

Set outside the Cotonera Lines, which protected the Knights' Three Cities (see page 42), Żabbar was given the name *Città Hompesch* after the Order's last Grand Master, who was the city's patron. The grandiose **Hompesch Arch**, or **Żabbar Gate**, stands on the outskirts of the village, and was dedicated to the Grand Master in the year of his surrender of Malta to Napoleon. Mainly a residential area and agricultural centre, Żabbar boasts a fine church, **Our Lady of Graces**, whose attached museum features paintings given as offerings for survival at sea.
Bus route from Valletta: 18

◆
ŻEJTUN

The ancient town of Żejtun has probably been inhabited since before the Punic age, and Roman remains have been excavated in the grounds of a local girls' school. When St Paul visited Malta, the villagers here refused to convert to Christianity; they are said to have stamped their feet so stubbornly that he put a curse on them and they were condemned to have flat feet forever. That is why the locals are known as *Tasaqajhom catta*: the flat-footed.

Żejtun has been a parish since the 15th century, and its two parish churches are the most notable buildings: the parish church of **St Catherine** has some of Lorenzo Gafà's best work, with a splendid dome and ornate interior; while the old parish church of **St Gregory**, extended by the Knights of St John with an incongruous Renaissance portal, is one of Malta's oldest surviving medieval churches. In the 1960s, during restoration work, several long secret passages were discovered under the roof; within these, the remains of about 80 people were found – possibly refugees from a pirate attack.
Bus route from Valletta: 26

Żabbar Gate, known as Hompesch Arch after the last Grand Master

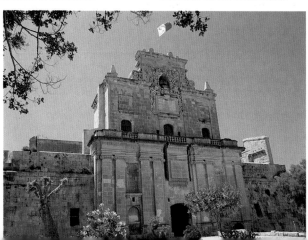

NORTH AND NORTHWEST MALTA

The northwestern corner of
Malta takes you away from busy
resorts and into remote farming
country, bounded by the
strange rock formations and
sandy bays of the coastline. A
long escarpment known as the
Great Fault divides this area
from the more populous parts of
Malta, and the remains of major
prehistoric temples can be
found here.

WHAT TO SEE

◆
GĦAJN TUFFIEĦA
Thanks to UNESCO funds, the
Roman *thermae* (baths) on this
ancient site beyond St Paul's
Bay were extensively restored
in 1961. The name means 'the
spring of the apple tree' and
enough remains to give you a
good idea of layout and
function, including mosaic
floors. The site is about a mile
(1.6 km) from Għajn Tuffieħa
Bay, a sandy beach where
swimming is possible.

*Ranks of colourful umbrellas
provide shade for sun-seekers to
stretch out and enjoy the view at
Mellieħa Bay*

MELLIEHA BAY
This small town on Marfa Ridge
overlooks one of the best sandy
stretches in Malta. From here
you can see the islands of
Comino and Gozo in the
distance and, to the left, the **Red
Tower**, built by the Knights to
guard the Ridge in 1649.
Mellieħa was one of the original
10 Maltese settlements given
parish status in 1436, though it
was later abandoned and not
re-established until 1841, since
which time the neck of land
beyond the bay has become a
popular tourist area. To the
Maltese, though, Mellieħa is a
place of pilgrimage, for in the
grotto of the old **parish church**
there is an ancient fresco of the
Virgin Mary, said to have been
painted by St Luke, and
certainly venerated for
centuries.
Bus route from Valletta: 43

◆
MĠARR

Egg-sellers raised the funds to build the **Church of the Assumption** here, and commemorated their achievement by adding an egg-shaped dome.

The main reason for a stop at this rural village is the ancient site of **Ta'Hagrat**, two prehistoric temples probably dating from the third millennium BC.

About a mile (2km) to the east, near the village of Żebbieh, are the few remains of the temple site of **Skorba**, where excavations in the 1960s revealed items from several stages of prehistory. Before the temples existed, this was a Neolithic village settlement, and the different styles of pottery found here gave their names to the Grey Skorba (3600BC) and Red Skorba (3400BC) periods of the Neolithic Age.

Bus route from Valletta: 46

◆
QAWRA

Qawra is very much a tourist area these days: hotels and restaurants have sprouted since its initial development in the 1960s. One restaurant is housed in **Qawra Tower**, one of the 14 towers erected by Grand Master Martin de Redin (1657-1660), who became famous during his brief period of authority for the number of castles and fortress towers which he built at his own expense. The better known examples are **Delimara Tower** and **Għallis Tower**, near Salina Bay (see page 54).

Bus route from Valletta: 49

◆◆
ST PAUL'S BAY

At this large, heavily developed tourist area there are holiday homes strung along the shoreline as well as hotels, villas, restaurants and watersport centres, all scattered between the district's sand-fringed ports. The resort area stretches for 3 miles (5km) from Xemxija to Qawra, and within its boundaries are the village of **Buġibba**, which has itself mushroomed into a fully equipped resort, and the tourist centre of **Mistra Bay**.

It was on the rocky islands of **Il-Gzejjer**, at the entrance of St Paul's Bay, that the apostle's ship was shipwrecked in AD60; the story is recorded in detail in the Acts of the Apostles (New Testament). Several of the sites here relate to this episode: the parish church of **St Paul** is said to stand on the site where St Paul threw a viper into the fire; and near the innermost curve of the bay, **Għajn Rasul**, or **Apostle's Fountain**, is said to be the spot where he struck a rock which miraculously spouted drinking water for the survivors of the wreck.

Protecting the harbour of St Paul is the restored **Wignacourt Tower**, constructed for Grand Master Adrien de Wignacourt in the 17th century.

Despite the development which has taken place here, this is an area which has retained much of its former charm, and the surrounding countryside is still worth exploring. Hikers might want to follow the trail from **Wardija Heights** to the **Grotto of San Martin**, or enjoy the agricultural scenery of the **Pwales Valley**.

To the southeast of the bay is the 17th-century church of **San Pawl Milqi** (St Paul Welcomed), built on the site of an earlier chapel and said to mark the location of Malta's first bishop, Publius' villa, where St Paul was a guest.

Bus routes from Valletta: 43, 44, 45, 52

◆◆
SALINA BAY

This bay takes its name from the salt pans which have been used commercially for centuries. At the head of the bay, which is protected by two of Grand Master de Redin's 17th-century towers, **Għallis** and **Qawra**, is

the **John F Kennedy Memorial Olive Grove**, which has a small playground; and behind it are some temple ruins. The main points of interest at Salina Bay are the **Tal-Lunzjata Chapel and Catacombs**, on the Naxxar road. The chapel dates from the 16th century, but the well preserved catacombs are 6th-century and have some interesting carvings and decorations. The central burial chamber may have been a family tomb; there are plainer tombs in the surrounding catacombs.

Bus route from Valletta: use the 54 to Naxxar or 52 to St Paul's Bay.

A statue on St Paul's Island celebrates the apostle's visit

CENTRAL MALTA

Central Malta, an area of pleasant towns and gentle foothills, was once the main orange-growing country, focused around the ancient 'Three Villages' of Attard, Balzan and Lija. Long, low stone walls extend across the landscape, where scattered inland communities were formed by islanders fleeing from coastal pirate raids.

WHAT TO SEE

◆
ATTARD
Attard and its neighbours, Lija and Balzan, are commonly referred to as the 'Three Villages' and are grouped around a once thriving area of orange groves. Attard's only worthy monument is its 17th-century parish church of **St Mary**, an impressive Renaissance-style building designed by Tomasso Dingli, which has a very fine carved façade.

Four miles (7km) away from Attard are the **San Anton Palace and Gardens**. You can not go inside the 1625 palace, which is the official residence of Malta's President, but the shady gardens, with their sub-tropical trees and flowers and a small zoo, make a refreshing spot, with the peaceful charm that only a stately garden can provide. They were planned by Grand Master Antoine de Paule in the 17th century – the palace was designed as his country residence – and are the setting for annual fruit and flower shows.
Bus route from Valletta: 74

◆
BALZAN
Stop here if you like churches: there are several attractive examples in this historic village. The baroque-fronted **Church of the Annunciation**, with its Spanish-influenced design, stands in the main square; and the pretty little **Church of St Roque**, with its decorated doorway, was built in 1593 and is dedicated to the protector of plague victims; it is located in Three Churches Street, along with the 15th-century **Little Church of the Annunciation**, and a church dedicated to **St Leonard**, which is privately owned.
Bus routes from Valletta: 40, 74

◆
LIJA
The third of the 'Three Villages' is a quiet community which has many typical Maltese houses. The church of **St Saviour**, built by Giovanni Barbara in 1694, is worth seeing for its ornate painted interior. Look out for the **Lija Tower**, on Transfiguration Avenue; once part of a private garden, this beautiful landmark now stands proudly in the middle of the busy road. **Tal-Mirakli Church** (Our Lady of Miracles) is a short distance from the village, where Preti's altarpiece is the main feature, designed for Grand Master Cotoner when the church was reconstructed in the 17th century.
Bus route from Valletta: 40

◆
MOSTA
Most visitors to this village, a couple of miles inland from the

northwest coast, come to see
the vast circular church.
Volunteers built **St Mary's**
around the smaller church
which originally stood here,
laying the first stone in 1833 and
following the design of local
architect Giorgio Grognet de
Vassé. St Mary's is remarkable
for its huge unsupported dome,
123 feet (37m) in diameter, one
of the world's largest and built
without scaffolding. It also has a
remarkable history: in 1942 a

*The massive dome of St Mary's
dominates the village of Mosta*

wartime bomb pierced the
dome during a service and
landed on the church floor
without exploding. Two other
bombs had hit the dome, but
rebounded – again landing
safely. The bomb which fell
through the roof, since defused
of course, is exhibited in the
church museum.
Bus route from Valletta: 53

◆
NAXXAR

The name Naxxar means 'to dry
out': the story goes that St Paul's
clothes were dried out here
after his shipwreck.

Naxxar is mostly a residential
and agricultural area, whose
history as a parish goes back to
the 15th century. The fine parish
church, **Our Lady of Victories**,
was designed by Tomasso
Dingli in 1616. Note the two
clocks on the outside of the
towers: these are quite a
common feature in Malta. One
gives the correct time but the
other is a fake, set at a fixed
hour. The superstitious belief is
that the devil, being confused
by two different times, will not
disturb those who are taking
part in the service.

The Knights built several
watch-towers in this district,
such as **Gauci's Tower**, behind
the 17th-century church of **St
Paul** in nearby San Pawl
Tat-Targa, and the **Torri
tal-Kaptan** (Captain's Tower,
1558), inside which la Valette's
coat of arms is carved. Naxxar's
fairgrounds are the setting for
Malta's annual International Fair,
during the first fortnight of July.
Bus route from Valletta: 54

◆◆
SIĠĠIEWI

Now a wealthy farming village,
Siġġiewi was founded in the
15th century and later bestowed
with the secondary name of
Città Ferdinando after Grand
Master Ferdinand von
Hompesch, the first German
Grand Master and the Order's
last Grand Master of all.
The parish church of **St Nicholas**

Spanning the church's vault . . .

has a partly 19th-century
exterior, but is richly baroque
inside – the work of Lorenzo
Gafà in 1675. Near the church,
in Quajjied Lane, several of the
houses still have 'Judas holes' –
peepholes which were once
common features in Maltese
buildings.

The **Villa Sant' Cassia** in St
Margaret Street is a
17th-century building which was
once the Palace of the Secretary
to the Inquisition.

West of Siġġiewi, in Wied
Girgenti Valley, is the elegant
Inquisitor's Summer Palace. The
Inquisitor was brought to Malta

. . . the ornate dome at Naxxar

to put down heresy and settle arguments between the Grand Master and the Bishop. Built in 1625 by Inquisitor Visconti, it is said to have been the scene of many lavish parties. It is also said that the staff lived in caves further down the hill, so that they shouldn't embarrass the Inquisitor. There is an 18th-century chapel adjoining the palace.
Bus route from Valletta: 89

◆
ŻEBBUĠ

A town of handsome churches at the centre of Malta. The most imposing building is the church of **St Philip** (1599), which is believed to have been designed by Vittorio Cassar, son of Gerolamo Cassar, who was largely responsible for building Valletta. St Philip bears many of the Cassar Senior trademarks, including the remarkable dome. The town's other churches are **St Roque**, Żebbuġ's oldest, built in the late 16th century; the 18th-century churches of **Our Lady of the Angels** and the beautifully decorated **Tal l'Abbandunati**; and **Tal Hlas**, with its screened wrought-iron windows, through which the priest could safely officiate during pirate attacks.
Bus route from Valletta: 88

WESTERN MALTA

Malta's highest ground is found on the western side of the island, where sheer cliffs drop to the sea. The ancient capital of Mdina grew up on this commanding territory, but most of the area is isolated farming countryside with terraced fields and small villages.

WHAT TO SEE

◆
DINGLI

Dingli is a tiny village situated at Malta's highest point on Gebel Ciantar, 830 feet (253m) above sea level, in an area of irrigated fields and orchards. The attraction here is the superb view from **Dingli Cliffs**, a dizzying drop to the sea. On the edge of the cliffs sits the isolated **Madalena Chapel**, a typical wayside place of worship. The small stone plaque on the wall indicates that criminals could not use this chapel as a sanctuary, as they could the larger Maltese churches. Similar warnings appear on many chapels; they date from the early 17th century, when the Grand Master decided that the church should limit its protection.

There are some lovely walks along the top of Dingli Cliffs; look out to sea for a view of the islet of **Filfla**, steep and rocky, three miles (5km) offshore. The island used to be a target for Royal Navy gunnery practice, which broke up the rock surface, revealing many ancient fossils. Today it is a bird sanctuary, favoured by storm petrels and shearwaters.
Bus route from Valletta: 81

Terraced fields at Dingli Cliffs

◆◆◆
MDINA

Known as The Silent City, not only for its intriguing, secretive narrow streets, but because no cars are allowed here, the old city of Mdina was Malta's first capital. It stands in a splendidly commanding position, 700 feet (213m) high, overlooking the plains and hills to the sea, and was probably inhabited as long ago as the Bronze Age. In Roman times the capital, then known as Melita, was much larger and took in the neighbouring town of Rabat. The name Mdina was given by the Arabs, who fortified the promontory in the 9th century, separating it from Rabat. Described in the 15th century as the *Città Notabile*, Mdina served as the Bishop's See and the seat of the Administrative body known as the *Università*.

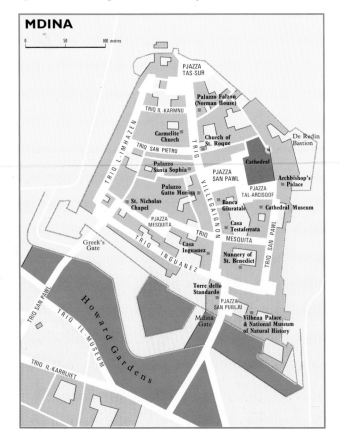

MDINA

0   50   100 metres

PJAZZA TAS-SUR

Palazzo Falzon (Norman House)

TRIQ IL-KARMNU

Carmelite Church

Church of St. Roque

De Redin Bastion

Cathedral

Palazzo Santa Sophia

PJAZZA SAN PAWL

Archbishop's Palace

Palazzo Gatto Murina

PJAZZA TAL-ARCISQOF

St. Nicholas Chapel

Banca Giuratale

Cathedral Museum

PJAZZA MESQUITA

Casa Testaferrata

Greek's Gate

TRIQ MESQUITA

TRIQ SAN PAWL

Casa Inguanez

Nunnery of St. Benedict

TRIQ L-IMHAZEN

TRIQ SAN PIETRU

TRIQ VILLEGAIGNON

TRIQ INGUANEZ

Torre dello Standardo

PJAZZA SAN PUBLJU

Mdina Gate

Vilhena Palace & National Museum of Natural History

Howard Gardens

TRIQ SAN PAWL

TRIQ IL-MUSEUM

TRIQ IL-KARRIJIET

Only when the Knights decided to build Valletta as their capital did Mdina become known as the *Città Vecchia*, or old city. The city has long been a home for the élite: Publius, Malta's first bishop, converted to Christianity by St Paul, lived here; and many of the older aristocratic Maltese families continue to make their homes here. Mdina boasts several restaurants, shops and a small guest house, all tucked away so as not to spoil its medieval atmosphere.

The city walls are a mixture of Roman, Byzantine, Arab and Norman work. Two ornamental 18th-century gateways, built by de Vilhena, provide access to the city across a bridged moat, the main entrance being the **Mdina Gate**. Just inside is the **Vilhena Palace**, built in French style, probably by Giovanni Barbara, and named after the 18th-century Grand Master for whom it was designed. Originally this was the Magisterial Palace, housing the city's administrative offices; it is now a **Natural History Museum**. Opposite the palace is the 16th-century **Torre dello Standardo** (Tower of the Standard), from which warnings of invasion were given.

Mdina's main thoroughfare, **Triq Villegaignon**, takes you right through the city to its fortified edge. It runs a relatively straight course, but many of the short, narrow streets of this 500-square-yard (418 sq m) settlement were built crooked to prevent the shooting of arrows. **Casa Inguanez**, on Triq Villegaignon, is the home of Malta's oldest aristocratic family,

The ancient city of Mdina

who governed the city before the Knights took over. King Alphonso of Aragon stayed here in 1432, and part of the house dates from 1350.

Off Triq Villegaignon, in **Pjazza San Pawl**, is the magnificent **Cathedral** (Co-Cathedral of St John with that of Valletta; see page 38), believed to occupy the site of Publius' former house. The original 11th-century church on this spot was destroyed by an earthquake in 1693, and what you see today, begun in 1697, was the masterful work of Lorenzo Gafà. Of particular note are the intricately carved heavy wooden doors through the vestry, the fresco of the Shipwreck of St Paul by Mattia Preti in the apse, and a silver processional cross which, it is said, the Knights brought to Malta from Rhodes.

Outside the Cathedral, to the right of the Archbishop's Palace, the former Seminary now houses the **Cathedral Museum**, well worth seeing, for it contains a lot of items saved from the old church. You will see some exceptional 15th-century marquetry, once part of the old choir, the bishop's carriage and various Papal Bulls, as well as Punic and Roman remains. You will also be thoroughly enchanted by the coin collection, which provides a sort of monetary trip through the ages. Upstairs there are various 16th- to 18th-century paintings from European schools of art. More interesting are the Durer woodcuts and engravings by Rembrandt, Piranesi, Van Dyck and Goya, and some of the exquisitely illuminated choir-books date from the 11th century. The **Palazzo Santa Sophia**, reputedly Mdina's oldest house, is found on Triq Villegaignon, and near the end of the street is the **Palazzo Falzon**, or **Norman House**. The lower section (14th- to 15th-century) has only slits for windows, while the upper section has attractive double-arched medieval windows. None of the old Mdina houses had windows; but they did have light and air, because they were built around courtyards. The thick outer walls were actually two walls with rubble fill-in designed to keep the interior cool. The Palazzo Falzon now houses paintings, furniture, pottery and antiques in a private museum (open Monday to Friday, 09.00 to 16.30 hrs). At the end of Triq Villegaignon is **Pjazza Tas-Sur**, which gives a spectacular view over the plain to Valletta.

Bus route from Valletta: 80

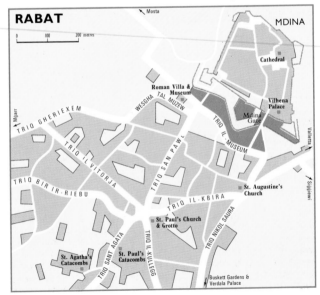

♦♦♦
RABAT

Until the Arabs built their
bastions around Mdina, Rabat
was a suburb of the capital; it is
certainly as old as Mdina, and
evidence from tombs found in
the vicinity suggest that it was
settled in Phoenician times. The
main features of interest in this
pleasant town are its catacombs
and Roman remains. Of the
latter, the principal site is the
Roman Villa and Museum,
beyond Howard Gardens
outside Mdina's Greek Gate.
Inside this pink stone building
are the remains of Greek,
Carthaginian and Roman
Tombs, with the items found
inside them, such as the large
stone 'olive pipper' used in
Roman times and, in the *atrium*,
delicately executed original
mosaics attained by a technique
called *vermiculatum*.

St Augustine's Church, in the
centre of Rabat, has a massive
barrel-vaulted interior and rose
windows which show the
Gerolamo Cassar style, for this
was the first major church to be
designed by him; it was built in
1571 and foreshadowed his
work on St John's Co-Cathedral
in Valletta.

On Parish Square, in the heart of
the town, **St Paul's Church** was
the first parish church in Malta
to be built to a Latin cross plan.
It was founded in 1575, but
rebuilt in 1692 by Lorenzo Gafà.
Mattia Preti designed the main
altarpiece, and there are
paintings by Preti and two
Maltese artists, Erardi and
Marulli. Underneath the
sanctuary is the **Grotto of St
Paul**, which can be lit up for a

few cents. St Paul is believed
either to have sheltered or to
have been imprisoned here for
some time and local legend
insists that no matter how much
stone is taken from the cave (the
sick sometimes take scrapings
for their curative powers), its
size never alters. There is more
certainty in the claim that the
grotto was home to Giovanni
Benequas, who came to Malta to
join the Order of St John in 1600
and adopted the life of a hermit
instead.

Near the church, signs point the
way to the **St Paul** and **St Agatha
Catacombs**, typical of the
underground Christian
cemeteries used in the 4th
century. Early Christians used
catacombs extensively for burial
and as shrines; later, when the
religion became more
widespread, churches and
chapels were erected over
them. Within the maze of cool
galleries there are many *loculi*,
or recesses, where bodies were
placed, as well as canopied
table graves and tombs cut in
imitation of the Greek
sarcophagi. St Agatha is said to
have lived here briefly after
escaping from Roman
persecution in Sicily.

In the Bir Ir-riebu district of
Rabat, the **Abbatija tad Dejr
Roman Catacombs** include a
little chapel that was still being
used in 1535 and features
13th-century frescos of the
Crucifixion. When Saracen rule
and its persecution of Christians
came to an end, the religion
re-established itself and its
followers used their catacombs
for worship. The chapel opens
on to arched tombs and

A Rabat street, straight up and down

first-floor room where French soldiers were imprisoned in 1812, with a chess board carved by the prisoners into the stone floor.

Opening hours are 09.00-12.00 and 14.00-17.00 hrs on Tuesday and Friday; if you want to visit outside these hours, tel: 45 40 21, or write to the Officer in Charge, Verdala Palace, Buskett, Rabat.

Buskett Gardens, below, take their name from the word *boschetto*, meaning 'little wood'; this is Malta's most fertile green area, planted with orchards and vines, and was the place where the Knights raised their falcons for hunting. Today it is a public park, and the setting for the annual folk festival of *Mnarja*, a weekend of singing, dancing and bare-back riding in late June.

canopied table graves; food would be placed on the stone tables for mourners.

A few minutes south of Rabat, overlooking Buskett Gardens, is **Verdala Palace**. Verdala was designed by Cassar in 1586 and today hosts official guests of the government. It was built as a summer residence for the vain and worldly Grand Master Hughes Loubenx de Verdalle, a great lover of pomp and power. This luxury country retreat, surrounded by pines, became his lordly manor. A magnificent staircase leads up to the door of the square moated castle, and the view is marvellous. The interior includes frescos and paintings of de Verdalle and other Grand Masters, and a

A quarter of a mile (0.5 km) from Buskett Gardens, at **Clapham Junction**, dozens of the puzzling prehistoric 'cart ruts' run towards the cliffs like skid marks on a busy motorway. Some run off the cliff edge, serving to heighten their mystery: one theory is that they were made by Bronze Age 'slide' carts; another that they were carved as tracks for wheeled vehicles.

Rabat is a good place to shop, especially for 'Malta weave', a brightly coloured cloth. Just outside the town, at **Ta'Qali**, a former airfield, huts have been converted to workshops and showrooms for Maltese handicrafts.

Bus route from Valletta: 80

SOUTHERN MALTA

Some of Malta's most important prehistoric temple groups are found on the southern coast of the island. Old fishing villages are dotted around the shoreline, and fortifications stand guard over the southeastern inlets, once so vulnerable to attack.

WHAT TO SEE

◆◆◆
BIRŻEBBUĠA

This fishing village has developed into the south's seaside resort, sprawling from St George's Bay round Pretty Bay (aptly named) to Kalafrana, with good bathing beaches. There is a small 17th-century chapel of some interest, and you can see the remains of the **Pinto Battery**, built by the Knights, but the major attractions are the two nearby prehistoric sites.

On a hill just outside the village is the 250,000-year-old cavern of **Għar Dalam**. The cave is a trove of semi-fossilised remains of extinct species, such as dwarf elephants and dwarf hippopotami. At one time the sea covered Malta, and when it receded it probably left a land bridge to Sicily, which large animals used as a crossing. On the floor of this 'cave of darkness' you can see the clearly defined layers of earth in which weapons and pottery, some dating back to 5000BC, have been found. A collection of these items is to be seen in the museum above.

On the opposite side of a valley from Għar Dalam is the Bronze Age temple site of Borġ in-Nadur. Only traces are left now of what was a small temple, probably dating from 1400BC, as well as evidence of Bronze Age storage pits; and examples of the mysterious cart tracks can be seen on the sea shore. Borġ in-Nadur gave its name to a culture which flourished between 1450 and 800BC; excavations have revealed that bronze was used here – one of the rare examples of metal-working on prehistoric Malta.

Bus route from Valletta: 11

Birżebbuġa's busy harbour

SOUTHERN MALTA

◆
GUDJA

Church lovers come here to admire the three 17th-century buildings of **St Mary, St Catherine** and the domed **Virgin of Loreto**, with its arcaded gallery.

Just outside the village is the more interesting, simply designed church of **St Mary 'Ta Bir Miftuh'** (St Mary of the Open Well), one of the original parish churches of Malta, which used to serve the needs of the outlying hamlets, and pre-dates the era of the Knights of St John. West of Gudja, on the route from Valletta, is the small village of **Għaxaq**, where a house with exterior murals has become a unique and colourful island attraction.

Bus route from Valletta: 8

◆◆
HAĠAR QIM

A large and impressive megalithic temple site, high on the southern coast overlooking the sea, not far from the village of Qrendi. Haġar Qim (Standing Stones) is unique among Maltese temples because it is made completely of globigerina limestone, which was probably quarried near by. The slabs used for the outer wall are very large, including the biggest single stone used in any temple, measuring 22 by 10 feet (7m by 3m). Many of the stones have unusual details and complicated decorations: one pillar 'altar' found here shows a floral motif that does not appear on any other megalithic structures on the island.

Bus route from Valletta: 35

◆
KIRKOP

Together with its small sister village of Safi, Kirkop is closely associated with **Luqa Airport**, which is near the mainly rural 16th-century settlement (see page 113). The parish church here is dedicated to **St Leonard**, and a prehistoric standing stone, topped with a cross, can be found to the north of the village.

Bus route from Valletta: 34

◆◆
MARSAXLOKK

Marsaxlokk, whose name means 'harbour of the Scirocco' (the warm winter wind from the Sahara), is Malta's largest fishing village and its most picturesque, situated on the eastern part of Marsaxlokk Bay. People flock to its colourful seafront to see the brightly painted *luzzu* (fishing boats) bobbing in the harbour, and the pretty houses, against their yellow cliff backdrop, whose reflections shimmer in the bay's water.

The *luzzu* are the same shape now as they were in Phoenician times, and are traditionally decorated in red, blue and yellow, always bearing the bright, carved 'eye of Horus', a symbol used to ward off evil at sea, which may have been adopted from the ancient Egyptians. The fishermen continue to mend their nets, untroubled by tourists, but if you want to admire the scene peacefully, don't come at the height of summer.

It was here that the Corsair Dragut landed in 1565 at the time of the Great Siege, and it

Bright luzzu *at Marsaxlokk*

was here again, despite the addition of some defensive towers which can still be seen, that Napoleon disembarked in 1798. The old **St Lucien Tower**, a Knights' fortress, is these days a marine laboratory.

If you take the small road that leads to Delimara Point, where the lighthouse stands, you will pass Neolithic ruins at **Tas-Silg**, where a temple to Melkart, a Phoenician deity, once stood.

Bus route from Valletta: 27

◆◆
MNAJDRA

Set in lovely remote country, the three megalithic monuments of Mnajdra are a short downhill walk from Ħaġar Qim (see page 66). Like their neighbours, the temples stand on high ground facing the sea, but are better preserved, perhaps because the protective outer walls are made from blocks of coralline limestone, which is far stronger than the globigerina used for the interior. They are excellently proportioned, built in a semi-circle, and you can quite clearly see the symmetrically decorated stones and the **Oracular Chamber**, with its little square holes, possibly used by the priest to speak to worshippers outside the room. The smallest temple probably dates from about 2600BC; the other two are slightly later.
Bus route from Valletta: 35

The Blue Grotto is a geological and marine wonder

◆
MQABBA

Mqabba's large stone quarries
have provided easily worked
building material. There is a
lovely church here, and the
village boasts several
16th-century houses decorated
with Moorish motifs. On the
southern flank are the
Tal-Mentna Catacombs, where
many of the 5th-century
Christian tombs are decorated
with scallop shell carvings.
Bus route from Valletta: 35

◆◆
QRENDI

Qrendi is an ancient village that
dates from Phoenician times.
Among its several churches, the
most intriguing is the small
building dedicated to **St
Catherine Tat-Torba**, with its
odd 17th-century façade
fashioned out of stone slabs. The
most important monument is
Gwarena Tower, incorporated
into a wall on the outskirts of
Qrendi. The octagonal design of
the tower, with boxes sticking
out from the crenellations to
allow defenders to fire down on
the enemy, is the only one of its
kind on Malta.
South of the village, a natural
fault in the earth's surface has
produced an unusual feature
known as **Il-Maqluba**: a vast
natural hole where trees and
shrubs grow, which can be
viewed from a belvedere by the
church. Legend has it that this
was once a village, inhabited by
people so evil that even the
devil disliked them. He threw
the rock where the village stood
into the sea, where it formed the
islet of Filfla.

Qrendi is not far from the
prehistoric sites of **Haġar Qim**
(see page 66) and **Mnajdra** (see
page 68).
Bus route fromn Valletta: 35

◆◆
ŻURRIEQ

Żurrieq was one of the 10
communities on Malta given
parish status in 1436, and its
parish church, **St Catherine**,
built in 1634 and altered over
the centuries, boasts superb
Mattia Preti paintings. The
remains of a Punic tower stand
in a neighbouring garden.
Now privately owned, the
17th-century **Armeria** housed
weapons for local communities,
and another survivor of the
Knights' era, the **Xarolla
Windmill**, was one of several in
Malta funded by Grand Master
Cotoner, and is now the only
corn-grinding mill still in
operation on the island.
In the nearby abandoned
medieval village of **Hal Millieri**,
the **Church of the Assumption** is
worth seeing for its handsome
murals, and in the **Church of St
John the Evangelist**, a Roman
olive-crusher has been
converted into a font.
Just beyond the village, tucked
into a narrow inlet beneath the
cliffs, is a miniscule natural
harbour, where boats set off in
good weather for trips to the
Blue Grotto. This consists of
several caves, at their best in
the morning light, with glowing
reflections in the water of
colourful coral and minerals
embedded in the limestone.
*Bus routes from Valletta: 32, 33
and 34 to the village; 38 to the
harbour.*

GOZO

Gozo is only nine miles (14.5km) long and four miles (6.4km) wide at its widest point, with a shoreline measuring just 85 miles (137km). There is no airport, and the pace is slower and more peaceful than on Malta. Some say it's a pity tourists ever discovered that Malta was not the only island for a holiday, but so far Gozo has not been overrun by crowds. 'Calypso's Isle' is where, according to legend, the enchantress Calypso kept Odysseus in bliss for seven years. The attraction is still easy to understand when you see the island's neat terraces, green fields and wild flowers.

Unlike Malta, Gozo did not meet the rest of the world by trading, but relied on fishing and farming for a living. Farming is

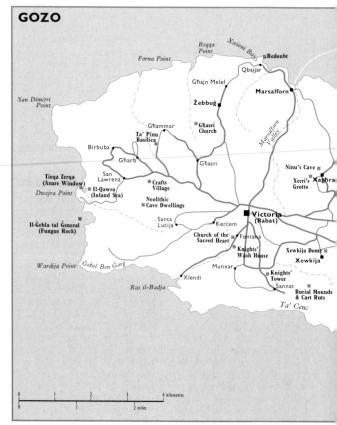

GOZO

still a vital part of the economy; Gozo supplies much of Malta's food and milk. The island is small and its land valuable, which is why the Gozitans have perfected a terrace-field system and built their villages on rocky hilltops. Most of the work still has to be done with hoe and scythe, and the donkey cart is still the most effective way for the farmers to transport their goods.

Prehistoric life and culture on Gozo was probably closely linked to that on Malta: the megalithic Ġgantija temples show a marked likeness to those at Tarxien and Haġar Qim. But Gozo has a distinct history of its own. From Roman times until the days of the Knights, the island was granted self-government and had equal status with Malta. Because it was less protected than Malta, Gozo

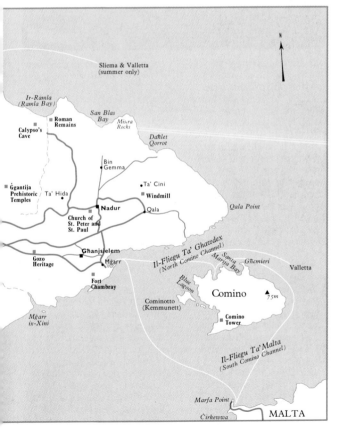

GOZO

suffered more from pirate attacks (they went on well into the 18th century) and at the hands of the Arabs and Turks. When the Turks attacked the island in 1551, they almost depopulated it, killing the older people, selling the younger ones into slavery, and seizing food reserves. But eventually communities were recreated, encouraged after the 17th century by the protection of defences built by the Knights. The Knights' influence can be seen in the numerous beautiful churches (about 29 parish churches and many chapels); it also changed the island's political status and Gozo came under the authority of the Grand Master.

Gozitans will tell you that they are quite different from the Maltese, and there is a friendly rivalry between the two communities: the Maltese will joke about the Gozitans' simple way of life, while Gozitans maintain that it takes one good man of theirs to put 10 Maltese

Gozo is renowned for its quiet pace and relaxed atmosphere

in their place. The crossing to Gozo, from Ċirkewwa or Sa Maison, is a short and pleasant one. The most active centre on the island is the capital, Victoria (Rabat); there is only one luxury hotel, but there are small hotels and restaurants in the little bays, where they will probably insist that you try the local wine and *gbejniet* cheese (goats' cheese bound with peppercorns). Buses do run on Gozo, but timings are unreliable. The villages operate their own buses, whose routes all converge on Victoria. A regular bus service to Mġarr is timed to meet the ferry and offers transport to Victoria and, in summer, to the resorts of Marsalforn and Xlendi. Taxis are widely available and relatively inexpensive, and of course this small area is accessible to walkers, although the terrain is more hilly than Malta's.

VICTORIA (RABAT)

The original name of Gozo's capital, Rabat, is Arabic, but the British named it Victoria for the Queen's Jubilee in 1897, and that at least avoids confusion with Malta's Rabat. There are good roads and bus services from the main port of Mġarr, which makes this a convenient venue for day trippers from the larger island.

Towering over the suburb is the hilltop citadel, which can be seen for miles; below, the main street, **Triq ir Repubblika** or Republic Street, is where the popular St George's Day and Assumption horse races begin; it leads past **Rundle Gardens** (named after the early 20th-century governor, Sir Leslie Rundle, and scene of the August Feast of Assumption fair and agricultural show) to the shaded central square, **Pjazza Idipendenza**, or **It-Tokk**, bordered by tiny shops and hole-in-the-wall bars, and the 18th-century **St James' Church**. *Tokk* means a place where people gather together, and this is always a very busy square, full of morning shoppers at the open-air market or evening promenaders, but it is at its most colourful on *festa* days, when religious statues and garlands are brought out. The maze of winding alleyways behind the square are well worth exploring, and on your way to the citadel you will find sweaters and lacework (hand-made lace is a celebrated island craft) displayed outside some of Victoria's tiny shops.

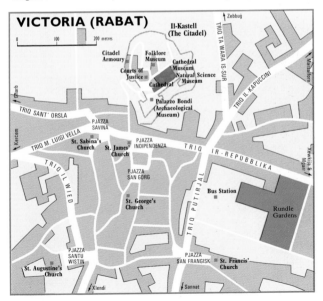

VICTORIA (RABAT)

Il-Kastell (The Citadel)

Zebbug

0   100   200 metres

Citadel Armoury
Folklore Museum
Cathedral Museum
Courts of Justice
Natural Science Museum
Cathedral

TRIQ TA WARA IS-SUR
TRIQ IL-KAPUCCINI
Maltaflorm

Palazzo Bondi (Archaeological Museum)

Għarb

TRIQ SANT' ORSLA

Kerċem

TRIQ M. LUIGI VELLA
PJAZZA SAVINA
St. Sabina's Church
St. James' Church
PJAZZA INDIPENDENZA

TRIQ IR-REPUBBLIKA

Xewkija & Mġarr

TRIQ IL-WIED

PJAZZA SAN ĠORG

St. George's Church

Bus Station

TRIQ PUTIRJAL

Rundle Gardens

PJAZZA SANTU WISTIN
St. Augustine's Church

Xlendi

PJAZZA SAN FRANGISK
St. Francis' Church

Sannat

WHAT TO SEE

◆◆◆
IL-KASTELL (THE CITADEL)
Also known as Gran Castello, the citadel was built on a bluff in the 15th century in defence against Turkish and Corsair attacks, and is reminiscent of the ancient Maltese capital of Mdina. Although it was strengthened after the brutal 1551 Turkish attack, there were so many subsequent invasions that the citadel dwellings were

A defence against pirate attack, the Citadel is strategically sited

abandoned. Restoration of these is under way. Climbing the steps to the ramparts, you will realise how strategic a position this was, on a hill in the centre of the island with an uninterrupted view to the sea. A walk round the ramparts should take about 20 minutes.

In the citadel is the lovely old **Cathedral**, designed by Lorenzo Gafà between 1697 and 1711. As is often the case in Malta, the austere stone façade hides an elaborate interior full of coloured mosaic tombs and a floor inscribed with Latin mottoes and family crests. The most interesting aspect of this cathedral, however, is what appears to be its domed ceiling. In fact it is a brilliant *trompe l'oeil* by Italian painter Antonio Manuele to disguise the fact that the roof is flat. (A dome had been planned, but there were not enough funds to complete it.) Before leaving, visit the **Cathedral Museum**, which contains sacred ceremonial items and several paintings including works by Giuseppe Hyzler, Michele Busetti and Tommaso Medion.

Just outside, to the left of the cathedral, is the **Palazzo Bondi** (Bondi Palace), once the home of a distinguished local family and now containing the **Archaeological Museum**. The objects on display range from prehistoric to Angevin discoveries, along with a model of the megalithic Ġgantija temples and one of the phallic symbols found there. Exhibits also include Roman amphorae and a headless 1st-century BC statue of a woman.

ST GEORGE
Pjazza San Gorg

This handsome baroque church stands on its own square and is ornately decorated. Though the roof is quite new, the original church was built some time before 1673, the year in which it was enlarged and improved as thanks for escaping the plague. The most striking painting is that of St George by Preti, set above the altar; George stands with his foot poised in victory on the dragon's head. The paintings on the dome are the work of Battista Conti of Rome, and there are also paintings by Giuseppe Calì and Stefano Erardi. There is a rather grisly relic of St Clement housed in the church.

Environs

◆◆
DWEJRA

In southwest Gozo, near Dwejra Point, there is a large outcrop of rock called **Il-Ġebla tal-Ġeneral** (General's Rock), also known as Fungus Rock. The fungus in question was a rare plant which grew here, highly prized by the Knights for its power to heal dysentery and haemorrhages. So valuable did they consider this plant that it was often presented to visiting nobility, and was kept under constant guard. Any attempt to steal it carried the death penalty – not that it was easy to reach: the Knights had to construct a hoist on the **Qawra Tower** in order to obtain it. The rock's Maltese name was adopted after an Italian general in charge of quarrying it during the Middle

Ages, who fell off the steep side and was drowned within arm's length of the shore.

Not far from the rock is another natural phenomenon called the **Inland Sea**, which is a fresh seawater pool reached via a natural tunnel. Strong swimmers can swim through the cave channel; or you can get there by fishing boat. The huge archway of rock which stands over the sea at Dwejra Point has been created by sea-breakers over thousands of years: a rocky ledge, about 328 feet (100m) long, rests on two massive columns, each about 130 feet (40m) in diameter, thus creating a 'window' through which the blue waters may be seen beyond. For centuries it has been known to the Gozitans as **Tieqa Zerqa** (Azure Window).

Fontana from the fields

◆
FONTANA
This village to the south of Victoria on the road to Xlendi is noted for its **Church of the Sacred Heart** and a public **wash house,** built by the Knights over a natural spring to supply water to the local inhabitants.

◆
GHARB
If Gozo has the perfect village then this is it: a peacefully pretty little place of pastel-coloured houses, about two miles (3km) northwest of Victoria. Several of the old buildings have ornately decorated balconies. The village is dominated by the **Parish Church of the Immaculate Conception**, fronted by statues of *Faith, Hope* and *Charity*, and displaying an altarpiece by Gio Nicolo Buhagiar, given to the church by Grand Master de Vilhena.

◆◆
IR-RAMLA
Gozo's best sandy beach is a long expanse along the northern shore, backed by low cliffs between Xagħra and Nadur. At one end of the bay are the underwater remains of a **Roman villa** and at the other a **redoubt** erected by the Knights.

◆◆
MĠARR
If you come to Gozo, you have to come to Mġarr. The approach to this southeastern port is worth a photograph: brightly painted *luzzu* bob up and down in the little harbour; church belfries grace the surrounding hills, including that of the majestic **Our Lady of Lourdes** church;

and the ramparts of **Fort Chambray** keep watch on the waterfront. The fort was originally planned by Grand Master Vilhena, but it was such an ambitious project that not until the French Knight Jacques François de Chambray provided private funds was it finally completed in 1761; and it was never developed into a town, as had originally been intended.

On the road between Mġarr and Victoria, the **Gozo Heritage** might be worth a stop: here, with the help of life-sized sculptures, some of them electronically animated, Gozo's historic events are retold (open: Monday to Friday, 10.00-17.00 hrs, all year).

Ir-Ramla is an attraction for sun worshippers and archaeologists

◆◆
MARSALFORN
Since it became a popular north coast bathing spot, this has not been the tranquil fishing village which it once was. The sandy spit and rock ledges near the hotel here get especially crowded, but the setting is picturesque. Marsalforn, whose name means Harbour of Bakeries, was favoured by the wealthier Gozitans long before foreigners discovered it. Two small bays lead from the village – **Qbajjar** and **Xwieni** – and a Knights' **redoubt** stands on a finger of land which juts out between them.

◆
NADUR

A large town on the eastern side of the island, situated 500 feet (152m) above sea level, Nadur's Arabic name means 'summit'. The local parish church is dedicated to **Saints Peter and Paul**: built by Bonici in the 18th century, it houses the relic of St Coronatus.

◆
QALA

This village, whose name is Phoenician for 'harbour', is a simple country place to the east of Nadur, whose 11th-century chapel was enlarged in the 17th century to become the **Sanctuary of the Immaculate Conception**; take a look at the 17th- and 18th-century drawings of ships on its outer walls. To the north of Qala is Gozo's last working **windmill**, and further on there are coves where you can swim.

◆◆
SANNAT

A **Knights' Tower** guards the approach to this small village on the southern coast, which is mainly noted for its lace-making. The rocky plateau behind Sannat, **Ta'Cenc**, is a beauty spot where awesome cliffs drop 590 feet (180m) to the sea. Almost hidden in this location is Gozo's only 5-star hotel, cleverly designed to fit in with its surroundings. A track leads to the almost inaccessible beach of **Mġarr-ix-Xini**, recommended for snorkelling. The Ta'Cenc area is well known for prehistoric cart tracks, possibly cut by hand by Bronze Age inhabitants.

◆
TAL-LUNZJATA VALLEY

Once the Knights' hunting ground, this remains the greenest part of the island, beyond the little village of Kercem, which is a short distance west of Victoria. Tucked under the cliff stands one of Gozo's oldest chapels, the **Chapel of the Annunciation** (1347, rebuilt in the 17th century).
Situated on the other side of the valley is the medieval **Knights' Wash House**, where the residents of Victoria would collect their water supply in barrels.

◆◆
TA'PINU BASILICA

This strange, somewhat isolated church and shrine stands by itself between Għammar and Għarb, on the western part of the island. It was actually built this century, in the 1920s, and looks rather incongruous, but it incorporates the site's original 16th-century chapel, which can be seen at the far end along with its original paintings and votive tablets. The old chapel, which was named after the pious caretaker nicknamed Pinu who looked after it in the 17th century, has become a place of pilgrimage. Its miraculous reputation dates from 1883, when a peasant woman and her friend both heard the voice of the Virgin Mary urging them to pray for the friend's desperately ill mother – who then recovered. In 1932, a year after it was consecrated, Ta'Pinu was given basilica status by Pope Pius XI.

◆◆◆
XAGĦRA

Excavation of the plain on which this village stands, about 2 miles (3km) northeast of Victoria, has produced a wealth of prehistoric finds. In the village itself, beneath two private buildings, are two caves with stalactites and stalagmites: **Ninu's Cave** and **Xerri's Grotto**. The 19th-century parish church in the main square was built in thanksgiving for the end of the plague which had caused the village to be sealed off. (The plague had been carried from Malta by a man who had hidden his clothes instead of burning them on arrival, as ordered.) The main attraction here is the **Ġgantija** temple complex, an amazing group of megalithic structures not far from the village (about a 10-minute walk). An exact date for the complex, which comprises two temples and a large forecourt, cannot be given: estimates vary from 280BC to 4000BC. The gigantic rocks weigh several tons and rise to 20 feet (6m), and it is still a mystery how they were moved with only the primitive tools of the period. According to myth it was a female giant, Sansuna, who brought them here on her head from Ta'Cenc. Inside the temples you can still make out the libation holes in the floor, an oracle hole and blocks carved with spiral decorative motifs. The fireplace in one of the apses might well have been used to shelter an 'eternal' flame. A large phallic symbol, found on one of the blocks, is now in the Archaeological Museum, Victoria. Note the

Ġgantija – built by a goddess

holes in the altar block of the bigger temple, possibly used during sacrifices. Some believe there to be an underground temple beneath Ġgantija, similar to the Hypogeum on Malta (see page 47), but if so it has yet to be discovered.

At the northeastern corner of Xagħra Plateau (overlooking Ir-Ramla) is another legendary place: **Calypso's Cave**. The myth is actually much more impressive than the cave, which is little more than a gloomy hole reached via a narrow staircase. In *The Odyssey*, Homer describes how Odysseus was enticed by Calypso, a beautiful nymph, onto the island, where they lived in the cave for seven years before she was ordered to send him home by Zeus.

◆◆
XEWKIJA

Xewkija is a plain village to the southeast of Victoria, but its church, **St John the Baptist**, is awesome. Built this century by local volunteers, it has a vast dome which was meant to rival Mosta's (see page 55), but is actually somewhat smaller.

◆
XLENDI

This is a popular place to stay on the southern coast, where you can take advantage of the sandy beach, sheltered beneath towering cliffs. Xlendi is still quite a modest little fishing hamlet with plenty of character, despite its appeal to visitors and developers, and is only a two-mile (3km) trip from Victoria.

COMINO

Comino is the smallest inhabited island of the Maltese archipelago, just one square mile (2.6 sq km) in size. Only a few farmers live here and there is one hotel (open summer only). There is no traffic, no noise and not a lot to do, other than while away the hours swimming and snorkelling in the crystal clear bays. A regular ferry service from Malta and Gozo allows you to make a day's visit. The island has its regular guests, who come back year after year to enjoy the clean air, scented by wild flowers and herbs (the island's name stems from cumin, a herb which once grew here in abundance).

Comino Tower was built in the 17th century by the Grand Master Alof de Wignacourt to protect the Gozo channel against pirates. It offered a clear view of the next tower in each direction – on Malta and on Gozo – so that messages could be signalled from one end of the archipelago to the other. The pirates, however, discovered the perfect hideaway, in the sheltered **Blue Lagoon** at the nearby uninhabited islet of Cominotto. Today the lagoon is particularly popular with visiting yachtsmen, who moor here for lunch and a few hours' tranquillity.

Comino: small is beautiful

PEACE AND QUIET

Wildlife and Countryside on Malta and Gozo
by Paul Sterry

Although Malta and Gozo are densely populated and intensively farmed, there is still a surprising amount of wildlife and scenery to be found. Many parts of the coasts are fringed with dramatic sea cliffs, the home of small colonies of breeding seabirds and focal points for migrants. Inland, small agricultural fields, surrounded by stone walls, are characteristic, but areas of maquis and garigue (typical Mediterranean habitats of open country), wet flushes in valley bottoms and small patches of woodland add variety. Even built up areas are not without

Cacti outside Mdina city walls

interest: parks and gardens attract birds and other animals which like scrubby habitats. It has to be said, however, that Malta's wildlife interest is decidedly seasonal. Flowers are at their best in late winter and early spring, while the best birdwatching is to be had during spring and autumn migration times. It is also at these times that the mass slaughter of birds for which Malta has a justifiably ugly reputation takes place.

The Coast
The southwest shores of Malta, as well as much of Gozo, are bounded by dramatic cliffs. Elsewhere around the islands, bays and natural harbours can

be found, combining to make a varied and interesting coast. Although a few coastal flowers survive in this harsh environment, the wildlife interest is largely confined to birds, but here they suffer greatly at the guns of Maltese hunters.

A characteristic bird of the cliffs is the herring gull. Elsewhere in Europe, they have pink legs but here it is the yellow-legged race that occurs. Herring gulls have grey backs and a powerful yellow beak with black and red markings at the tip. Blue rock thrushes sing their mellow song from rocky outcrops, their nests unfortunately being subject to the attentions of collectors, who take the young for the songbird trade. Male blue rock thrushes live up to their name: they have deep blue plumage. However, females are a more sombre brown colour.

Truly oceanic seabirds also breed around Malta and Gozo. Storm petrels nest on the offshore island of Filfla ,as do Manx shearwaters and Cory's shearwaters, which also breed on cliffs around the main islands, such as at Ta'Cenc, on the south coast of Gozo. These species only return to their burrows at night, often spending the day far out to sea. However, during periods of strong onshore winds they come close to shore – try Ras ir-Raħeb, west of Rabat, and Għar Lapsi on the south coast – and this is especially true of Cory's shearwaters. The islet of Filfla was formerly used for naval target practice. Although at the time this had a devastating effect on the breeding seabirds, the rubble created greatly favours the storm petrels, which nest in profusion now that the firing has ceased.

Maquis and Garigue

Prior to man's arrival on Malta and Gozo, the islands would have been cloaked in woodlands, probably comprising evergreen oaks and aleppo pines. With the exception of a few remnant areas, most notably the aleppo pine woods at Buskett Gardens, itself not exactly natural, this habitat has been replaced by agricultural land. Buskett lies near the coast on the road south from Rabat. (Park in the village or catch a bus from Valletta.) A marked trail leads east through the gardens and up the valley of Wied il-Luq. Reafforestation schemes are under way around Xemxija and Delimara.

In a few uncultivated areas that have escaped the attentions of goats and sheep, natural vegetation has been able to recolonise. The vegetation is not, however, the woodland that was once found here, but instead forms distinct habitats known as *maquis* and *garigue*. *Maquis* vegetation is made up of bushes, low-growing plants and the occasional tree. Species of broom, gorse and heathers are very common, with rosemary, sages, myrtle, rock-roses and cistuses adding colour and a unique combination of scents. *Garigue* vegetation usually occurs on stony, well-drained and often lime-rich soils. A good example of this habitat can be seen at Għar il-kbin on the track south from Buskett. In spring, the bare soil is studded with low-growing plants such as grape hyacinths, French lavenders, thymes, hyssop, fritillaries and star of Bethlehem. European whip snakes, leopard snakes and catsnakes are sometimes seen in early spring. These reptiles are justifiably wary of man because they suffer greatly from unnecessary killing.

Spring Flowers

Visitors to Malta and Gozo during the summer months might be forgiven for thinking that the islands are barren and lifeless. With the exception of irrigated areas, much of the vegetation is brown and parched, but return in spring and things are rather different: green plant life is abundant and colourful flowers are everywhere.

The seasonality in the growing and flowering periods of many of the plants is linked to the seasonal rainfall. May until September are virtually dry months, but from October until February the rainfall contributes to the mild, wet winters. After the first downpours of autumn, the plants produce new growth and in spring – February until May – a succession of flowers appears.

Many of the seasonally appearing plants survive the dry summers in the form of underground bulbs and tubers, and a large number of the species are similar to or identical with horticultural varieties. Among them are crocuses, tulips, fritillaries and squills. They can be found growing alongside lavenders, vetches, poppies, grape hyacinths and thistles.

Rock-roses in the pink

PEACE AND QUIET

Agricultural Land

Small arable fields, surrounded by low stone walls built from rubble from the land they enclose, are a feature of the Maltese landscape. Terraced hillsides and extensive irrigation add to the area used for farming and a wide range of crops is grown. Although agriculture is often incompatible with wildlife, a surprising range of plants (particularly arable 'weeds') and animals still persist alongside man in Malta due to the comparatively small-scale nature of the operations. There are good fields on the west coast around Victoria, Dwerja and Xlendi.

In a few areas, trees such as olives, carobs, figs, lemons and oranges are grown, but the most widespread crops are fodder vetch, potatoes, wheat, grapes and tomatoes. Where not sprayed, the leaves of potatoes are food for the caterpillars of the death's head hawk moth. The moth itself is impressive enough – a five-inch (13cm) wingspan and a skull-like marking on its back – but the

The death's head hawk moth caterpillar

caterpillar is particularly striking. The size of a man's middle finger, it is pale green with beautiful diagonal stripes down the body and a shiny, black 'horn' at the tail end. One of the commonest birds of agricultural land is the Spanish sparrow, which forms large flocks on occasions. Male Spanish sparrows are attractively marked with a striking black throat and breast, a chestnut cap and white cheeks. Females by comparison are rather sombrely marked.

Wetlands

Wetlands of any sort are few and far between on Malta and Gozo. Small-scale irrigation schemes have created reservoirs, and valley bottoms sometimes harbour wet scrub full of common reeds and giant reeds. The Chadwick Lakes – actually reservoirs – northwest of Rabat occasionally hold a few wildfowl and there are salt pans at Salina Bay on the north coast of Malta near Buġibba, that attract a few species of birds, but the only wetland of any real note is at Ghadira which, thanks to the actions of the Maltese Ornithological Society, is now a reserve. Ghadira lies in northwest Malta on the west side of the road which borders Mellieħa Bay.

Cetti's warblers often breed in the damp areas as well as around Ghadira. This site attracts a few black-winged stilts and avocets but more frequently encountered species on migration are little-ringed plovers, ringed plovers, Kentish plovers, little stints, curlew sandpipers, common sandpipers, wood sandpipers, ruffs, redshanks and greenshanks.

Towns and Gardens
Although towns are not usually good for wildlife, many of the more mature gardens and parks provide cover for scrub-loving birds and other animals, and buildings are a refuge for some species.

Spanish sparrows commonly nest under eaves in houses and outside the breeding season may form large roosts in towns. Geckos – both Moorish and Turkish geckos are found on Malta – live inside the houses and serve the useful function of keeping down insect numbers. Careful observation in more rural areas may even reveal a chameleon. These curious reptiles were introduced about 100 years ago and are now widespread although, regrettably, they are widely collected for the pet trade.

Chameleons remain motionless in the vegetation. Despite their striking shape, their green colouring helps give them good camouflage. Valletta is now home to the last colony of Algerian whip snakes, a rare and endangered species which occurs nowhere else in Europe. This snake can grow to a length of 39 inches (100cm). The grey-brown back is mottled with darker markings and there is a dark 'v' behind the head.

Bird Migration
Without doubt, the spring and autumn migration seasons are the highlights of the bird-watching year on Malta and Gozo. Visitors fortunate enough to be on the islands during the months of April to June or September and October can expect to see a wide variety of birds, although the exact species and numbers present cannot be guaranteed, being highly subject to prevailing weather conditions.

The reason why so many birds pass through Malta on migration lies in its strategic position. A large number of bird species that breed in northern Europe only spend the summer months there, crossing the Mediterranean and heading south to Africa for the winter. Malta is a convenient stopping-off point between mainland Europe and north Africa, especially if weather conditions suddenly change for the worse. With clear skies and light winds, large numbers of both day and night migrating species will fly straight over, but if, for example, they encounter a

PEACE AND QUIET

cold front and rain, they may
become grounded. Some birds
do not migrate as far as Africa
and large numbers of song
birds from northern Europe
spend the winter on Malta and
around the Mediterranean in
general.

Migrant birds are best looked
for in the habitats with which
they are normally associated on
their breeding and wintering
grounds. Larks, tree pipits,
tawny pipits and red-throated
pipits are often found in
ploughed fields, along with
wheatears and thrushes. Grey
herons, little egrets and squacco
herons are occasionally found
around the coast and sometimes
around the few areas of marsh
such as Ghadira.

In the early mornings, patches
of scrub and gardens may
harbour garden warblers,
icterine warblers, sedge
warblers and subalpine
warblers as well as flycatchers –
spotted, pied and collared
flycatchers have been
recorded. Birds of prey are day
migrants and honey buzzards
and marsh harriers are the most
frequently seen species. The
valleys of Wied il-Luq near
Buskett, Wied Znuber and
Mtahleb on Malta and Xlendi
and Mġarr ix-Xini on Gozo are
particularly rewarding.

Hunting

One of the saddest aspects of
Maltese life is the trade in
caged birds and the wholly
unnecessary slaughter of tens of
thousands of birds by hunters.
While at one time these may
have supplemented the local
diet, the birds are shot

nowadays mainly for so-called
sport, and the corpses and
spent cartridges are a
heart-breaking sight to anyone
with any sympathy for wildlife.
The Maltese Ornithological
Society puts the number of birds
shot or trapped each year in the
millions. As examples, more
than a million finches are
thought to be trapped annually,
and around 100,000 robins,
200,000 thrushes and several
thousand birds of prey and
herons are shot each year. With
some species, such losses may
be disastrous and will
undoubtedly have long-term
effects on the population as a
whole. This is especially true
when one considers that Malta
is by no means the sole culprit
in this slaughter, since birds are
shot and trapped in most
Mediterranean countries. Also,
migratory birds are facing
numerous other threats, such as
loss of breeding and wintering
grounds.

Thankfully, recent legislation
affords a degree of protection to
some of these species but, of
course, the laws need to be
properly enforced. Much of the
credit for recent changes in the
law, and the creation of the
reserve at Ghadira, are due to
the Maltese Ornithological
Society. If visitors are still able
to watch birds on Malta in years
to come, it will be due in no
small way to their actions.

For further details on
conservation and anti-hunting
legislation on Malta, the **Maltese
Ornithological Society**, PO Box
498, Valletta, Malta has
published an excellent book on
the birds of Malta.

FOOD AND DRINK

Fish of the day!

Seafood naturally predominates on the Maltese islands' menus. You will be offered *pixxispad* (swordfish), *merluzzo* (red mullet) and *tunnagg* (tuna), often cooked the Maltese way: with tomatoes, green peppers and onions. You will also find prawns and lobster, but don't expect them to be cheap. Octopus and squid are highly popular and are served on their own or in salads, stews or curries. One fish which is a speciality of the island is the *lampuka*, in season between late August and November. The firm, white-fleshed *lampuki* breed in the Nile delta and swim west in shoals, growing fatter as they go: they can grow to two feet (0.6m) long or more by December.

Beef and lamb tend to be cooked in casseroles with potatoes and onions; and speciality restaurants might serve braised pork, sweetbread and brains. The national passion is for *fenek* (rabbit), which is often served cooked in red wine with garlic.

Garlic, herbs and olive oil are popular ingredients in Maltese cooking, and there is a distinctive Italian flavour to many menus, although dishes have been adapted to the Maltese style. Specialities include the Maltese version of minestrone, *minestra; timpana*, a pasta-based dish not unlike lasagne; and *ravjul*, a Maltese ravioli stuffed with ricotta cheese. Several restaurants specialise in Italian cuisine, but Malta's cooking is as international as its history: Arab influences are responsible for *mezzes* and kebabs, for instance, and the British won't have to worry about going without their fish and chips. Potatoes, tomatoes, onions and green peppers are popular vegetables, along with such items as beans, aubergines and courgettes.

Imported cheese, many of them Italian, such as ricotta or Bel

FOOD AND DRINK

Paese, are frequently used. The local cheese, made of goat's milk, is called *gbejna*, and is a Gozo islanders' speciality; it tends to be rather dry; it may also have peppercorns added. For a snack, try the savoury *pastizzi*, small puff pastries filled with ricotta or meat. The local bread is traditionally made by hand from an age-old recipe, and is baked in wood-fired ovens.

The most common summer fruits are fresh figs, plums and peaches; tangerines and lemons are widely available, and oranges are grown from December to March.

Desserts and cakes are particularly delicious on Malta, where the islanders are very sweet-toothed. Menus will include pastries with honey and nuts, biscuits with almonds, Italian style ice cream, dates wrapped in pastry and flavoured with lemon and brandy; and at festival times, special cakes and confectionery include the Easter *figolli* (iced biscuits flavoured with lemon

and almond), and *prinjolata*, a creamy almond sponge concoction made during Carnival, before Lent.

The following list describes a selection of Maltese specialities, some of which have already been mentioned:

Bragioli: beef olives. Thin slices of steak rolled around a mixture of minced meat, olives, hard-boiled egg, bacon, breadcrumbs and parsley.

Brodu: broth. A basic Maltese soup, prepared from boiled beef flavoured with celery, marrow and turnip. (Another popular soup is the *aljotta* (fish soup), made with boiled fish and flavoured with onions and mixed herbs.)

Brungiel: stuffed aubergines, usually filled with minced meat, tomato paste and semolina.

Bzar Ahdar: green peppers stuffed with a variety of fillings.

Fenek biz-Zalza: rabbit stew. The rabbit is first fried in fat and wine, then stewed with potatoes, peas, onions, mixed

Spoilt for choice at the bakery

herbs and more wine.

Kusksu: pasta mixed with green beans or peas and onions.

Minestra: a variation of the Italian minestrone (vegetable soup) but thicker.

Quarnita: cuttle fish or octopus stew, cooked with olives, onions, nuts, raisins, peas and wine in a rich casserole-style dish.

Ravjul: Maltese ravioli, filled with ricotta and served with tomato sauce and Parmesan cheese.

Ross il-Forn: baked rice, cooked with minced meat, eggs and cheese.

Soppa ta' L-Armla: Widow's Soup. Rather a hearty soup with egg and fresh cheese, peas, cauliflower and mixed herbs.

Timpana: a long, thick type of macaroni, layered with hard and soft eggs, liver, onions and a variety of other ingredients, and baked in a pastry case.

Torta tal-Lampuka: slices of *lampuka* fish, fried, then covered with pastry and baked along with tomatoes and onions, olives, parsley, peas and cauliflower.

Drinks

Thanks to the Italian influence, most establishments serve good *espresso* coffee, and thanks to the British, there's no shortage of tea. Familiar brands of soft drinks are readily available; *kinnie* is a very sweet local drink.

Malta has its own brewery, Farson's, which makes a range of good, inexpensive beers, and there are plenty of imported brands. Imported wine is also available, but Malta's own wine is passable and cheap, although the reds tend to be rather heavy and sharp, especially on hot days. The brands to look for include Marsovin Special Reserve and Lachryma Vitis. Gozo produces its own wine, which is far stronger than the Maltese brands.

Restaurants

Malta does not have many exclusive restaurants – but neither does it charge exclusive prices. What you will find is a range of pizza parlours and snack bars, tea rooms and cafés, bistros and informal restaurants and one or two first class establishments. Some of the most stylish restaurants are located within hotels.

The government classifies restaurants, and almost all of them offer both *à la carte* and *table d'hôte* menus. The set or tourist menu normally comprises a three course meal.

Restaurant hours and closing days vary, but most places close one day during the week. As a guideline, a bistro is likely to open all day long, between 10.00 and 23.00 hrs; tea rooms and cafés might open for breakfast at around 08.00 hrs. Some pizzerias open 11.00 to 14.00 hrs and again 17.00-23.00 hrs and snack bars tend to open 10.00-14.00 hrs and 16.00-23.00 hrs. Most restaurants open for evening meals 19.00-24.00 hrs or 20.00-23.30 hrs, and some open for lunch (about 11.00-14.00 hrs). A number of ethnic restaurants have opened in Malta, especially on the main island, where Chinese and other Far Eastern cuisine is popular.

FOOD AND DRINK

Inexpensive Restaurants

Hamburgers, seafood or steak are on offer at **Al Fresco**, at St George's Bay, B'Bugia for very reasonable prices.
Chains, 90 Grenfell Street, St Julian's (tel: 33 11 14), need not cost a lot if you select wisely, and **Hunter's Tower**, Wilga Street, Marsaxlokk (tel: 87 13 56) is an old favourite. Also try **Il-Brigante**, on Ball Street, Paceville (tel: 51 17 74); **Pappagall**, Triq Brittanja (Melita Street), Valletta (tel: 23 61 95); and **Rumours**, 113 Xemxija Hill, St Paul's Bay (tel: 57 36 78).

Maltese Restaurants

Ta'Kolina, at 151 Tower Road, Sliema (tel: 33 51 06), is a must for anyone interested in the local cuisine; it seats 60.
Il-Fortizza, on Tower Road in Sliema (tel: 33 69 08) is a local restaurant on a larger scale, with room for 200.

Pubs

One of the legacies of British rule is the popularity of pubs, where you can have a drink and often a snack in a cordial atmosphere at no great expense. Some eating houses have adopted the pub style, serving simple meals in unpretentious surroundings. The **Barrel and Basket**, St Augustine Street, Rabat (tel: 45 42 46) has space for 50, and the long-established **Buskett Roadhouse** in Buskett Gardens, Rabat (tel: 45 42 33) is good for a cheap and cheerful atmosphere, as is the **Rose and Thistle**, 49 Paceville Avenue, Paceville (tel: 51 64 94). Sliema has many pubs serving food, and there are several pubs in St Julian's.

Seafood and Grills

Arches, 113 Main Street, Mellieħa (tel: 57 34 36) has a good reputation and can seat 100 customers. Other restaurants worth visiting are **Barracuda**, 194 Main Street, St Julian's (tel: 33 18 17) and **The Carriage**, The Strand, Sliema (tel: 33 45 84), a small place (it seats 20) with a first class reputation. **Giannini**, 23 Windmill Street, Valletta (tel: 23 71 21) is a fairly new international restaurant with a superb view and thoughtful service, much appreciated by lunchtime business people. **La Loggia**, 39 Mrabat Street in Sliema (tel: 51 34 76), seats 60 and is quite popular.
The **Medina** at 7 Holy Cross Street (tel: 45 40 04) includes seafood on its menu, although it is not a speciality; this is a popular place to eat, with décor of white walls and wrought-ironwork. **Palazzo Pescatore**, on St Paul's Street, St Paul's Bay (tel: 57 31 82), has space for 120 and offers a range of fish dishes; and **San Guiliano**, 3 St Joseph's Street, St Julian's (tel: 23 15 53) has an attractive view over the harbour. **Winston's**, 16 High Street, Sliema (tel: 33 45 84) used to have consistently high standards, but tends to be variable nowadays.

Snack Bars

The **Café Cordina**, 244 Triq ir Repubblika (Republic Street), Valletta (tel: 23 65 05) is highly recommended.
Another good place to try in Valletta is **Café de la Vallette** at City Gate (tel: 23 77 04). **La Belle Époque**, 34 Tigne Seafront,

Sliema (tel: 33 13 72) is pleasant and **Pizzeria Bologna**, 59 Triq ir Repubblika (Republic Street), Valletta (tel: 62 61 49) is highly regarded.

Speciality Food

One of the best places to go for Chinese food is **China House**, 8 Spinola Road, St Julian's (tel: 33 50 21); this is Malta's original Cantonese restaurant, but the menu features European and vegetarian dishes, too. Over the years many more such establishments have opened, though not all have stayed the course. One that has achieved notability is the **Peking**, opposite the Hyperion Hotel in Qawra (tel: 47 31 14), which serves a combination of Cantonese and Szechuan food. You could also

Imbibe the atmosphere of Valletta in Victoria Square

try the **Marco Polo**, on the Dragonara Road, St Julian's (tel: 33 19 95); and a less expensive option is the **Shanghai**, 4 Ross Street, Paceville (tel: 31 79 05), where there's a vast menu of Chinese delicacies and a take-away service, but space for only 36.

Other recommended ethnic restaurants include **Kyoto** (for Japanese fare), 131 Spinola Road, St Julian's (tel: 33 43 98); the **Taj Mahal** (for Indian dishes), 122 The Strand, Gzira (tel: 33 92 46); the **Bouzuki** (Greek), Gort Street, St Julian's (tel: 33 69 24); and **Sumatra** (Indonesian), 139 Spinola Road, St Julian's (tel: 80 19 22).

SHOPPING

Do not expect to find large department stores in Malta: there is only one of any size, in Floriana. Most shops are small and fairly specialised, and you can take your pick from the outdoor markets and government-run or village handicraft centres. You may well find bargain prices in the markets and small Gozo stalls, especially if you are buying more than one item, but haggling is not customary here, so don't expect to cut down the asking price.

On the main island, the largest variety of shops is found in Valletta and Sliema, though choice has increased in recent years at all the resort centres. The main places to shop in Gozo are Victoria, Xlendi and Marsalforn. As a rule of thumb, Maltese shops are open six days a week 09.00-19.00 hrs, but they are likely to close for two hours at lunchtime and close on Sunday (there is a rota system). Internationally known labels are available – Body Shop, Benetton, Gucci and Cardin goods are sold in the major resorts – but the best buys are undoubtedly the locally produced handicrafts. At the top of the list comes **Mdina glass**, often in turquoise, though it is made in marbled shades of green and brown, too. Decorative items range from paperweights to pretty vases, bowls and ash trays – and the glass is all hand blown: you can watch it being made at Ta'Qali, but the glassware is on sale in shops throughout Malta.

Silver filigree work is another must: Maltese silver is reputed to be especially pure, and is fashioned into bracelets, rings and Maltese crosses.

Gold is also widely available: jewellery-making is a centuries-old Maltese craft. Many jewellers are located in Valletta, Sliema and St Julian's, and at craft showrooms such as the Malta Crafts Centre in Valletta, and the Crafts Village in Ta'Qali.

The **ceramics** industry has grown rapidly in recent years: items for sale at the craft centres tend to be in a rustic style, fired into blue or brown vases and dishes. You can be assured of their high quality.

Lace-making is a traditional skill, practised in many villages

Less expensive ideas might include decorative tiles, many of which feature Maltese motifs. Keep an eye out for **Malta stone**, a calcite onyx found in Malta and Gozo, and which is banded into cigarette and jewel boxes, book ends, ash trays, etc. There is a workshop at Ta'Qali which specialises in this craft.

If you like **wickerwork**, head for the alleys off Main Street in Ħamrun, where this industry has been flourishing for some time.

The Maltese are highly skilled in **wrought-ironwork**. Products range from lamps or candlesticks to tables and dramatic figures of the Knights in their full armoured regalia, which are made in a variety of sizes and have a variety of uses – such as concealing bottles of wine.

There are several **leather** factories in the vicinity of Valletta and customers can ask for a garment to be made up within a few days, or buy off the peg in one of the shops.

Woven material has a far longer association with the islands. Weaving was a thriving industry in the Bronze Age, and Maltese sailcloth became a staple export during the Roman period. Nowadays the colourful, traditional **Malta weave** appears as table linen, cushion covers, bags, furnishings and dresses.

Hand-made **lace** is a speciality on Gozo, where it is a cottage industry with a long tradition, although the young village women may be less inclined to enter the trade than their grandmothers were. The industry which started in the

Triq il-Merkanti, Valletta

17th century to provide churches with fine lace adornments has developed into a popular and marketable craft: all over Malta you will find lace on collars, providing a delicate fringe to a handkerchief or table cloth, or worked into a handsome shawl. Attractive crocheted and knitted sweaters come in several styles, from sleeveless tops in light, soft wool, to the bulkier, coarser variety with nautical designs. Cotton goods are now much more varied and widely available. Lace, crocheted and knitted items are all best bought on Gozo, particularly around Victoria or Xlendi.

Craft Centres

Malta Government Craft Centre
is situated at Dar-l-Annona,
Castille Square, Valletta (tel: 24
30 48), and here you will find a
wide choice of all the best of the
island's handicrafts. The centre
opens during standard Maltese
government museum hours (see
Directory, under **Opening
Times**).

The **Ta'Dbiergi Crafts Village**
(tel: 55 62 02) is a collective
centre of Gozo handicrafts,
which you will find at San
Lawrenze.

Ta'Qali Craft Centre is situated
on an old converted airfield just
outside Rabat, where huts have
been converted into
workrooms.

Most of the handicrafts
mentioned above may be seen
here in the making, and are
displayed for sale in the
showrooms.

The glass factory is particularly
interesting and you may find
bargains on the seconds shelf,
where prices are often as much
as 50 per cent less than those
for items which are unflawed.
Bus No 80, which runs between
Valletta and Rabat, passes very
close to the entrance of the
factory.

Unfortunately, the crafts centre
is closed at weekends, but you
can visit any time from Monday
to Friday between 10.00 and
16.00 hrs.

Markets

An open-air flea market takes
place during the mornings at
Valletta.

Some other towns also hold
occasional markets which are
worth looking out for.

ACCOMMODATION

The Maltese authorities are the
first to admit that they are
lacking in 5-star hotels, although
there are plans to develop
more. Sales and disputes have
caused the closure of some top
bracket hotels recently: at the
time of writing the **Phoenicia**, for
example, just outside Valletta, is
shut and due for extensive
refurbishment. The **Excelsior**,
near Valletta, and the
Dragonara Sheraton in St Julian's
(tel: 33 64 22) are both
reopening after periods of
closure, the latter with a new
wing and facilities which
include a watersports centre
and casino. Many of the other
existing hotels are applying for
building extensions.

The variety of 2- and 3-star
hotels is enormous, and there is
a broad choice of self-catering
complexes, holiday villages and
guest houses, so there is no
shortage of bed space.
(Applications for new hotels
below the 3-star category are
not being considered.) On the
main island, much of the
accommodation is sited around
Sliema, St Julian's and St Paul's
Bay. Apart from its one 5-star
hotel, Gozo accommodation
tends to be smaller and cosier –
most of it at Marsalforn and
Xlendi.

Comino only has one hotel,
which closes during winter.
Somewhere a little out of the
ordinary is the **Malta Health
Farm** in Tarxien (tel: 78 64 77/82
35 81), a small former hunting
lodge that caters for those
interested in health and fitness,
though its restaurant doesn't

only serve dietetic food, and its tiny bar is a popular gathering place.

Top Hotels

Officially, the island of Malta has four 5-star hotels, and the island of Gozo one. Widely recommended as the best option is the **Hilton** in St Julian's (tel: 33 62 01), currently the largest in the top bracket, with 201 rooms. It has a lively lobby bar, a night-time bar with live music and a highly regarded restaurant, and is located at the heart of one of the most active resorts.

The 182-room **Holiday Inn Crowne Plaza** in Sliema (tel: 34 11 73) offers a very good health and leisure club and has a discothèque in its own grounds. The genteel, stately 108-room **Phoenicia** in Floriana has been shut due to an industrial dispute and plans for refurbishment; it has a superb location, with views over Grand Harbour, and a high reputation, and may reopen boasting even more grandeur.

Gozo's **Ta'Cenc** (tel: 55 68 30) is a delightful hilltop hotel, whose 100 rooms are now all air-conditioned.

Four-Star Hotels

For an attractive location, you couldn't do better than the 105-room **Cavalieri** in St Julian's (tel: 33 62 55), which is popular with British guests. The 155-room **Corinthia Palace** in Attard (tel: 44 03 01) is a long-established hotel with its own health and leisure centre and the use of a lido at Qawra; and 5 miles (8km) away, the **Eden Beach** at St George's Bay (tel: 34 11 91), with over 100 rooms, is another well-situated hotel, and is part of the group which owns the Palladium

Ta'Cenc Hotel, Gozo

ACCOMMODATION

nightclub, Styx 11 discothèque and the Eden Super Bowl (see page 107).

If Sliema is your choice as a holiday base, the **Preluna** is recommended (tel: 33 40 01); it sits on the seafront promenade and has 281 guest rooms and a penthouse restaurant-cum-nightclub.

At Qawra, the best bet is the 420-room **New Dolmen** (tel: 47 36 61), situated on the Buġibba seafront, close to many tourist facilities.

Some people may feel that Marsaskala is a little too quiet for them, though the rocky bay is pleasant. The best choice here is the 350-room **Jerma Palace** (tel: 82 32 22), which offers a health centre and shared facilities with its sister hotels, **Corinthia Palace** and the **Mistra Village Complex**. The 164-room **Grand Hotel Verdala** (tel: 45 17 00) is another isolated spot, on its hillside position not far from Rabat, which is a 20-minute ride to most of the tourist attractions. Set on the seafront of Ċirkewwa, the 215-room **Paradise Bay** (tel: 47 39 81) is a reasonable choice; and the 64-room **Ramla Bay**, on the coast at Marfa, is excellent for families.

If you prefer to be at a distance from the seafront, the 149-room **Selmun Palace** (tel: 47 24 55) could be the answer. Located on high ground between St Paul's and Mellieħa bays, this hotel is set in the grounds of the 18th-century Selmun Palace, once occupied by a charity which ransomed slaves from North Africa.

There is no 4-star hotel accommodation in Gozo yet, but the **Comino Hotel** (tel: 47 30 51), on the island of Comino, does have this rating.

Courting Lady Luck at the Casino

Three-star Hotels

Sliema has a number of 3-star hotels, including the **Eden Rock** (tel: 33 55 75), the **Europa** (tel: 33 00 80), the **Marina** (tel: 33 64 61), the **Metropole** (tel: 33 01 88), the **Sliema** (tel: 33 63 14) and the **Regent** (tel: 31 87 64). Two of the best equipped hotels are the 100-room **Plevna** (tel: 33 10 31) and, a little further from the seafront, the 93-room **Imperial** (tel: 33 00 11).

Another place with a variety of 3-star properties is Buġibba, where you will find the small **Carolina** (tel: 47 15 36) and **Concorde** (tel: 47 38 31) hotels. The 175-room **Hyperion** (tel: 47 36 41) and the 60-room **Mediterranean** (tel: 47 14 61) both have gym facilities.

The 59-room **Miramare** (tel: 34 11 63) is a highly recommended hotel in St Julian's. For good family accommodation, try the 318-room **Golden Sands** (tel: 47 39 61), a stone's throw from a sandy beach at Ghajn Tuffieħa, and the 300-room **Mellieħa Bay** (tel: 47 38 44).

Among Gozo's 3-star options, the 50-room **Cornucopia** at Xaghra (tel: 55 64 86) is a comfortable hotel which has become one of the island's most popular establishments and retains its farmhouse character. Another favourite is the 92-room **Calypso** at Marsalforn (tel: 55 61 31), which is based on the seafront, and has a disco and a Chinese restaurant.

Inexpensive Hotels

One- and 2-star hotels are scattered throughout Malta and Gozo and almost all have restaurant facilities. Among the more notable examples are the **Central** in Mosta (tel: 44 89 47), which has an in-house hair salon; the **Cove** in St Julian's (tel: 33 50 62), which boasts a gym and dance floor; the **Tropicana** in Paceville (tel: 34 11 88), which offers watersports and dancing; the tiny **Duke of Edinburgh** (tel: 55 64 68) in Victoria, Gozo, and the even tinier **St Patrick's** (tel: 55 65 98), which has a lovely position on Xlendi Bay.

Guest Houses

Most Maltese guest houses are rather small: few can offer more than 10 rooms. One of the most appealing examples is the **Palazzo Costanzo** (tel: 45 63 01), with a prime position on Triq Villegaignon at the heart of Mdina, and a tremendous atmosphere. Others include **Ramla Lodge** on St Thomas Bay, Marsaskala (tel: 82 49 33); **Soleado** in Sliema (tel: 33 44 15) and **Xaghra Lodge** at Xaghra in Gozo (tel: 55 34 05).

Tourist Villages and Complexes

Purpose-built complexes of tourist accommodation come into first, second and third class categories. One of the best is **Mistra Village** at St Paul's Bay (tel: 47 39 44), which it overlooks. This apartment complex of holiday flats is very popular with families. Its amenities include a self-service store, disco, two children's pools as well as two for adults, and a sports centre. A large, modern resort centre is the **Suncrest** on the Qawra coast (tel: 47 54 70); known as a 'full service leisure resort', it has several restaurants, a leisure centre and

Cabaret time at Eden Palladium

415 rooms, suites and apartments. **Topaz**, in Buġibba (tel: 47 24 16), is another aparthotel with 170 varied units and facilities that include a fitness centre, two pools, pub, pizzeria and restaurant.

Gozo offers the **Peacehaven** self-catering apartments in Marsalforn (tel: 55 18 59), a short walk from the seafront and the Calypso Diving Centre, and the **Masri Court Rustic Villas** at Xaghra (tel: 55 26 33), which has use of a swimming pool.

NIGHTLIFE AND ENTERTAINMENT

Malta is not the place for a glamorous nightlife, plush clubs or international cabaret. The nearest things to Las Vegas are the flashing signs in front of the discothèques and the rattle of chips in the casino. But visitors should bear in mind that tranquillity is an essential part of the Maltese experience, and a glittering nightlife wouldn't fit the special character of the islands.

Despite listings to the contrary, there is only one authentic nightclub, and that's the 700-seater **Eden Palladium** in St George's Bay (tel: 31 98 89), part of the Eden Group's leisure complex. It has all the latest lighting technology, but seems to have set itself up as a revue bar-cum-cabaret with showgirls and dancers. It may yet raise its standards and star quality.

There are plenty of opportunities for dancing. Almost all the hotels have dance floors, either for evening use (with a live band or discs) or for weekly occasions. A few restaurants have their own small dance floors and there are some establishments which call themselves nightclubs where you can dance. There is no shortage of discothèques. One of the best is **Styx 11**, under the Eden Beach Hotel in St George's Bay: it's a large place with high-tech multicoloured laser lighting, good sound systems, a video wall, five bars, a snack bar and video games. It is regularly jammed with under 21s, especially at weekends, and is as popular with the locals as it is with visitors. Nearby **Axis** (tel: 31 80 78) is similar, and both are noisy and jumping from 22.00 to 05.00 hrs.

Others to look out for include **The Black Rose**, Qawra (part of the Dolmen Hotel); **Tigullio**, St Julian's (tel: 33 59 65) and **The Pharaoh's Den** (part of the Salina Bay Hotel). Several piano bars (also with small dance floors) have recently appeared in Malta's resorts, more geared to the over 21s.

Gozo has a few small discos, mostly in Victoria, Marsalforn and Xlendi. If in doubt as to where to go, ask at your local hotel or check the local paper or *What's On* guide. (Note that some discos close around 01.00 hrs.)

Cinemas are scattered throughout Malta, usually showing films in English or Italian, but don't expect recent releases. Gozo's cinemas are located in Victoria. Many hotels show films as part of their own weekly entertainment programmes. (They may well also include a folklore night during the week.)

For **theatre** entertainment, the best place to go is the **Manoel Theatre** in Valletta (tel: 24 63 89 for bookings), which has its own symphony orchestra and hosts international performers most of the year. Drama and ballet is staged, as well as opera and concerts.

A few plays and operas are presented in winter at Gozo's theatres; the major venues are the **Astra**, Triq ir-Repubblika, Victoria (tel: 55 62 56) and the **Aurora**, on the same street (tel: 55 69 74).

If you fancy dicing with Lady Luck, the **Dragonara Casino** in St George's Bay (tel: 31 28 88) is a must; it opens between 20.00 hrs and some time after midnight. Bring your passport and take your pick from American roulette, French roulette, Blackjack, Craps, *Chemin-de-fer* and the slot machines.

WEATHER AND WHEN TO GO

Malta has one of the highest sunshine records in Europe, and in summer it certainly does get hot, with average daytime temperatures between June and September ranging from 75°F to 90°F (25°C to 32°C); come prepared with sun cream, sunglasses and hat, particularly if you are very fair-skinned. Evening temperatures are generally cooled by sea breezes, so you may need to take some warmer item of clothing, such as a wrap or jumper. Be prepared for sticky weather in September and October, when the warm Scirocco wind blows in.

In the winter, strong winds bring in a cooler climate, with average November to March temperatures of 50°F to 70°F (10°C to 21°C).

The highest rainfall tends to be between October and January, though figures can fluctuate quite dramatically from year to year. Fog, frost, snow and ice

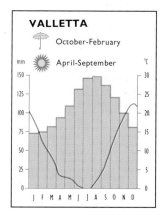

VALLETTA

October-February

mm   April-September   °C

are virtually unheard of. The best times to visit are spring and autumn, avoiding the uncomfortably hot high summer period.

Malta is not a dressy destination and, given its climatic conditions, light cottons – short-sleeved shirts, slacks and sun dresses – are the recommendation, although one or two establishments (the casino, for instance) may require men to wear a jacket in the evening. Shorts and swimsuits are perfectly acceptable in the resorts and at the beaches, but cover up to visit churches. This is a Catholic country, and the older generation tends to frown on short shorts, micro-minis, tank tops and other abbreviated garments worn in holy places. Topless and nude bathing are illegal, so don't strip when you sunbathe. If you plan to walk or take in the prehistoric sites, comfortable flat shoes are essential.

HOW TO BE A LOCAL

The welcome which St Paul received after his shipwreck on the island and the continuing celebration of his work there are good illustrations of some of the elements of Maltese life. The Maltese are generally kind and hospitable people. They are courteous socially and in business and, while astute in business dealings, with a keen eye to profit, the islanders' watchword is fairness. In return for hospitality, visitors are expected to show respect, and – as is usually the case

worldwide – a smile and a 'thank you' will go a long way. Religion is very important to the Maltese, Roman Catholicism being the religion practised by the overwhelming majority of the population. Churches are a source of great local pride, and the focus for celebrations of local holidays. Throughout Valletta you will see shrines and statues on street corners, and in some parts of the islands there are even shrines on the buses. Visitors are expected to dress modestly when they visit religious places. Bikinis may be a common sight on the beach, and shorts in the street, but topless and nude sunbathing are illegal. In country areas attitudes to dress are more conservative, and you may see older women wearing traditional dress – the *faldetta* or *ghonella:* a black cloak with a stiffened wide hood.

The Maltese are proud of their traditions, and this can be seen in aspects of every-day life. Over two and a half thousand years ago, the Phoenicians brought to the islands the habit of painting eyes on the prows of their boats as a talisman, and fishing boats today are still decorated with the 'eye of Horus'.

Despite their absorption of many different cultures, the Maltese have retained their own distinctive character – in fact, within the archipelago, there is a clear distinction between the Gozitan and the Maltese way of life, although many young people from the smaller island tend to leave its quieter, simpler life to find work on the main

Time to reflect at Marsaxlokk

island. Most islanders speak English and Italian, but Maltese is the official language, and any attempt at a few words or phrases will be taken as a gesture of courtesy.

The Latin influence on Maltese life is clear in the islanders' passionate and proud nature, their respect for the family and their great love of children, as well as in a hearty enjoyment of good food. It's an influence which is also evident in the heavy furnishings and ornate decorations to be found in many Maltese homes. But the Maltese can also be more English than the English in their manner of speech – particularly if they

have been educated abroad or have lived overseas.

You will find a combination of qualities – sometimes contradictory – in the islanders of Malta. Although they are a cosmopolitan people, their attitudes can at times seem insular; they can be frugal savers or frivolous spenders. And on top of an inherent caution, you may well find some adventurous behaviour: keep a look out for cars speeding down the middle of the road. Anyone driving on the left hand side at a stately pace is *not* likely to be a local.

CHILDREN

Because of the scarcity of sandy beaches (the best are in the north), some people would say Malta is not the perfect place for children. There are no Disney-style theme parks, and just one complex of water slides but no other man-made attractions specifically designed for kids. On the other hand, Malta might well be considered the ideal family holiday destination: the water is clean and unpolluted, and there are many shallow spots where the smallest child can swim and paddle safely. A number of family holiday hotels, such as **Golden Sands** (see page 97), offer children's facilities – playgrounds and pools, for example – and organise weekly programmes for youngsters. The Maltese love children, and numerous cafés and snack bars serve pizzas, hamburgers and ice cream.

Slightly older youngsters will find Malta an excellent place to learn watersport skills. Several watersport centres (both at and outside hotels) offer instruction in sailing, windsurfing and snorkelling, and conditions are first class for practising these sports (see **Sport**, page 112). As for the teenagers, they will find plenty of discothèques full of laser lights, videos and mind-bending sound, that are crowded with under 21s. Another good bet is the **Eden Super Bowl** at St George's Bay, where 20 bowling lanes are equipped with computerised scoring, and there are bowling facilities for young children.

Children of all ages will enjoy the fun of a *festa*. Countless religious festivals take place on summer weekends in the towns and villages, and there is always an element of fun, with parades, fireworks, donkey rides and a fairground atmosphere. The Maltese have a great love of fireworks and the villages compete against each other for the best displays, so you can be sure of a lot of razzle-dazzle. Another must, suited to all ages, is the audio-visual presentation *The Maltese Experience*, shown in several languages in an auditorium of the **Mediterranean Conference Centre** in Valletta (tel: 24 37 76), which gives an interesting history of the islands and a fascinating insight to Malta's background (showing times are as follows: hourly 11.00-16.00 hrs Monday to Friday, 11.00 and 12.00 hrs Saturday).

Parents with young babies will find Malta a suitable location. It shouldn't be difficult to obtain the services of a babysitter, either through your hotel or by looking through the local newspaper.

Well-known brands of baby foods and other baby goods are fully stocked on store shelves, so even the self-caterers should have no worries in this regard.

TIGHT BUDGET

You don't have to stay at a top hotel to enjoy a holiday in Malta, or even, for that matter, a 3-star hotel, since there are several alternatives, including holiday villages, aparthotels and guest houses (see **Accommodation**, page 97). Most of the better guest houses have a restaurant: by not having full board you pay less, but have the option of an evening meal, which can be better than having to clear out after breakfast.

Both Malta and Gozo have self-catering properties which may be rented by the week, and this can be an excellent choice when the budget is tight, whether it be in a villa, holiday flat or an aparthotel. You won't find large supermarkets in which to shop for supplies, but you certainly won't be short of the basics. Registered holiday accommodation (including self-catering and guest houses) is listed by the Malta Tourist Office by category, although there are some unclassified properties, either because they're new or because they're not officially rated. You can expect to pay about LM4.50-8.75 for bed only at a tourist complex, aparthotel or similar. If you are on an exceptionally tight budget, youth hostels are a bargain. Try the **Marsaxlokk Hostel** (tel: 87 17 09) and **St Francis Ravelin**, Floriana (tel: 22 44 46), both first class; or the **Paceville Hostel** (tel: 23 93 61); **Trafalgar-Buġibba** (tel: 64 04 12); or the **Youth Travel Circle**, Rabat (tel: 23 38 93), all second class. On Gozo there is a hostel at Għajn Sielem (tel: 55 93 61). Restaurant prices have risen recently as owners have tried to increase the choice or improve the quality of their menus, but that doesn't mean you have to pay a fortune for a meal. There is no shortage of pizza parlours, snack bars and cafés charging reasonable prices (see **Food and Drink**, page 90). In Valletta you will get value for money at the **Cordina Café** (one of the city's oldest), as well as an excellent cheesecake and coffee. **Hunter's Tower** in Marsaxlokk and **Il-Fortizza** in Sliema are also recommended. Unless you are on a tight timetable, Malta's bus service works very well for a very low price. Most towns and villages on the main island are connected with Valletta, where the main terminus is at City Gate. Village termini are generally near the parish church or main square. If you are unsure of which number you need or wish to enquire about departure times, ask at the kiosk at City Gate.

Some quick hints:

- Bed and breakfast is a simple and cheap option at guest houses (about LM3.50-5.50)
- A pasta dish costs less than steak or seafood
- Local wine is inexpensive; a glass can cost about the same as a cup of coffee
- Car hire is reasonably priced and useful, especially on Gozo
- Sharing the cost of fuel can be economical if you are travelling with a group
- Look for bargain seconds at Malta's craft centres (see **Shopping**, page 94)

SPECIAL EVENTS AND FESTIVALS

Almost any excuse will do for the Maltese to hold a party. National public holidays are ideal occasions, of course, and between May and October every town and village has a *festa*, or feast day, for its patron saint. The core of the event is religious, but it also involves packing in as much merriment as possible during the lead-up period, and on the special day itself. Much of the activity takes place on the weekend closest to the actual saint's day.

Not surprisingly, the local church is the focal point. For the *festa* it will be draped in red damask and filled with flowers. Its treasures are brought out for public viewing, along with a statue or holy relic of the saint. The façade of the church and the streets are lit with fairy lights and festooned with garlands, and flags are hung from house balconies. During the normal three- to five-day build-up, there are many preparations to be made and prayers to be said. On the feast day itself, the saint's statue is carried in procession through the streets as the church bells ring and brass bands play, while children throw confetti over the whole parade. Piety is combined with fun, as people stop to chat to friends or buy a candy floss on their way to the church. Concerts are often given in the main square and there will almost certainly be a fireworks display. The Maltese are specialists when it comes to fireworks, and the villages compete with each other to present the biggest and most dazzling display. The tourist office should be able to supply you with *festi* dates for the year (see **Directory**, under **Tourist Offices**).

Throughout the year, specialised fairs take place in the fair grounds at Naxxar, and there are several major sport events, such as the **Sicily – Malta Windsurf Race** in May and the **Four-Wheel Drive Rally** in November.

Several national festivals are popular occasions for celebration, including the following:

February

Carnival takes place in the period preceding Lent, and is the time when the islanders really let their hair down. In the villages, the families hold their own celebrations and children wear fancy dress and masks, but the main event takes place in Valletta, where there is a parade of colourful floats, folk dancing contests and fireworks. Carnival festivities have been held for centuries on the island and are still hugely popular occasions.

If you are feeling very fit, you may want to make a point of being in Malta in February for the **Marathon**. Since it was started in 1986 the Marathon has proved a successful annual event, which appeals as much to international runners as it does to local athletes. The distance is a 26-mile (42km) established route starting from the gates of Mdina and eventually finishing in the resort of Sliema.

March/April

31 March is a national holiday, celebrated with fireworks, parades and marching bands in Valletta and Vittoriosa.
Easter is more solemn, especially Good Friday, when processions of hooded *penitentes* carry holy statues through the town streets. Good Friday pageants are held in 14 different towns and villages, and life-size statues depict scenes from the passion and death of Christ. Men and women wear costumes to represent Old and New Testament characters. On Easter Sunday, early morning processions of the Risen Christ

Celebrating the Feast of St Philip

are held in several towns and villages (those in Vittoriosa and Cospicua are considered among the best), and it is still customary for children to have their *figolla*, a sweet made and sold during Easter, blessed during these processions. The *figolla* iced biscuit comes in different shapes, usually that of a lamb, basket or fish. Whatever your generation, if you are a scout (or have been), you can join in the annual **National Scouts Parade** in April. It takes place in Valletta, and representatives of groups from throughout the island march to lively band tunes.

June
The **Mnarja** is a popular festival which takes place at the end of June. Its name is corrupted from the Italian *Luminaria* (illumination): in the past the bastions around Mdina were illuminated by bonfires to mark the event. The celebration was originally a harvest festival, but it has become a night-long picnic held in Buskett Gardens, Rabat. On the eve of 29 June, vast quantities of fried rabbit and wine are consumed, and there are exhibits of agricultural produce, decorated carts and folk-singing competitions. On the following day bare-back horse and donkey races are held in the street leading to Rabat. The winners receive brocaded banners, which they take back to their local church.

September
The 8 September **Regatta**, held in Valletta's Grand Harbour, commemorates Malta's victories in the two Great Sieges of 1565

and World War II. Against the backdrop of Fort St Angelo, traditional colourful boats race against each other, manned by rowing teams hailing from the towns around the harbour. On 21 September, the **Commemoration of Independence Day** is celebrated with fireworks and parades.

November
The International Choir Festival has choirs from all over Europe.

December
Republic day (13 December) celebrates the founding of the Republic in 1974 with more fireworks, bands and parades.

SPORT

Malta is a very sports-conscious island: whatever sport you enjoy, you are almost sure to find it available here, albeit on a small scale. Many of the large hotels have sport and recreational facilities of their own, or, at the very least, have an arrangement with centres elsewhere. Obviously, watersports take high priority and are one of the most attractive reasons for a holiday here.

If you are based in Malta for some time and are an active sports enthusiast, it may be worth your while taking out a weekly membership, offered to tourists, with the **Marsa Sports Club** (tel: 23 38 51/23 28 42). This is the island's biggest sports centre, located about 2 miles (4km) south of Valletta. Here you will find the island's only 18-hole golf course (covering 5,600 yards (5,120m), par 68; resident professional coach), an international 18-hole mini golf course, 18 hard tennis courts (five of international standard, two floodlit at night; residential coach), five wooden-floored squash courts, an international cricket pitch, two coin-operated billiard tables, a fully equipped gym with qualified instructor, plus sauna and fresh water swimming pool (open mid-May to mid-October). Near by are the race track; polo grounds, football ground and rugby pitches. You might also enquire about using the **Union Club**'s facilities in Sliema (tel: 33 49 62), where there are tennis and squash courts, plus a beach facility at Tigné.

Archery
The **Malta Archer Association** (tel: 24 43 51) organises archery at the Marsa Sports Club. There is an international tournament in April. (Some of the larger hotels might also offer archery competitions as part of a weekly programme.)

Athletics
The **Malta Amateur Athletics Association** organises several events during the year, including road races, cross country and track and field events. The Athletic Championships take place at the Marsa Stadium track in May. Another major annual event is the **Malta Marathon**, held in mid-Feburary, which attracts a number of overseas runners. For further details write to Godwin Zammit, Brantwood Alley, 6 Main Street, Mosta.

Boating and Sailing
Naturally, as a Mediterranean island, Malta's boating facilities are excellent, whether or not you come in your own boat. You can rent anything from a small dinghy to a luxurious yacht. There are several good watersport centres where you may hire boats: good yachting facilities are available at Qawra, Marfa Bay, Marsamxett Harbour and Mellieħa Bay, and the **Malta Yacht Club** at Manoel Island (tel: 33 11 31) will be pleased to give advice about yacht charter (and does accept temporary members). **Ripard Larvan and Ripard** at Gzira (tel: 33 15 63) run a sailing school as well as hiring or chartering a full range of vessels in all sizes, both motor and sail.

Sailing regattas are regular events between April and November. Among the most important are the Comino regatta in June, the Malta – Syracuse keelboat race in July and the Rimini – Malta – Rimini yacht race in August.

If you are bringing your own boat, you will find that the **Yacht Marina** at Ta'Xbiex has stern-to-quay accommodation and other berths are also available at Msida Creek. Around 350 yachts may be berthed at Lazzaretto and Msida Creeks: facilities include electricity, telephone, weather forecasts, ship-to-shore radio, TV, water, bottled gas and compressed air.

Bowling
Eden Super Bowl at St George's Bay (tel: 34 11 96) is the best centre for 10-pin bowling, with

SPORT

Water sports off Mellieħa Bay

20 lanes and automatic computerised scoring. (It also features a fast food bar, cocktail bar and a pro shop with ball-drilling facilities and bowling accessories.) It is open every day, including Sunday, from 10.00 hrs to past midnight. Another 10-pin bowling centre, with five lanes, open all week, is located at Enrico Mizzi Street in Msida (tel: 33 23 23).

Clay Pigeon Shooting
Skeet shooting is popular in Malta, usually on Sunday mornings, when practice or competitive shoots take place: contact the **Bidnija Shooting Club**, 99 Dingli Street, Sliema or tel: 44 47 47/23 13 12 with enquiries.

Diving
Malta is considered a mecca for divers and snorkellers – all three islands have healthy waters and rich fauna. Rare and familiar fish are visible around the islands, including the *Anthias Anthias* (a species which has vanished from other parts of the Mediterranean). Obviously, the weather and sea situation will affect visibility, but you can reckon on an average of 98 feet (30m). Because of the clear visibility, this is an ideal destination for underwater photography, and the natural oranges and reds will come out at depths of 33 to 39 feet (10 to 12m) even without a flash. Diving is a year-round activity, because even in the severest winter the sea temperature

never drops below 55°F (13°C), and there are several sheltered dive sites. The seas around Malta are more or less tideless and underwater currents are rare, especially in summer.
To be able to make a dive, you need a permit, available from local health authorities. If you have never dived before, proper training is essential: courses are available at several centres and hotels, including the **Paradise Bay Hotel**, Čirkewwa (tel: 47 03 84); the **Jerma Palace Hotel**, Marsaskala (tel: 82 32 22); the **Calypso Hotel**, Marsalforn (Gozo) (tel: 44 61 32); and the **Comino Hotel** (tel: 47 30 51) on Comino.
The experienced diver will find that Malta is perfectly suited to night dives, and most of the diving schools include night diving in their programmes. You are unlikely to bump into tuna, dolphins or bonitos; if you do see them at all, it will be in winter. The most predominant

fish are amberjack, bream, damsel fish, red mullet, octopus, squid and stingrays. Occasionally, you might see moray eels and possibly John Dory. The following dive sites are recommended:
In the north of the main island, **Čirkewwa**, near the departure point of the Gozo ferry, has long been favoured for its impressive drop, from 26 to 98 feet (8 to 30m), its photographable arch and its numerous caves. As it is on the channel, visibility is also exceptionally good.
At the northeast point of Malta, **Aħrax Point** is ideal for beginners. A 10-minute snorkel will take you to a reef rich in marine life or to an underwater cave.
When winds prevent diving in other northeasterly areas, you might consider **Anchor Bay**, where entry to the water is from a pier.

About to plumb the depths

SPORT

At the northern tip of St Julian's
Bay, **Merkanti Reef**'s niches
house a variety of fish life which
will be appreciated by
underwater photographers. If
you are a strong swimmer, you
should reach it easily from the
land, but it may be more
comfortable to use a boat.

At the southern tip of St Paul's
Bay, **Qawra Point** is popular with
those who like a long dive.
Among the marine life to be
seen are various weird sponges.

At the fishing hamlet of **Għar
Lapsi**, on the western coast,
access to the water is easy, and
it only takes a few strokes to
reach a shallow system of
underwater caves. There is a
large reef area here, housing
the most typical Mediterranean
marine fauna.

A night dive is particularly
enjoyable at **Wied iż-Żurrieq**,
where crabs venture out of their
hiding holes.

Teeing off at Marsa golf course

On Gozo, **Reqqa Point** is the
northernmost tip of the
archipelago. This site offers
excellent diving *for experts:* the
entry is not easy and the swell is
likely to be strong. The reef
here consists of a parapet at 98
feet (30m), which drops to 197
feet (60m), although even at 50
feet (15m) you will be
surrounded by shoals of small
fish.

Another spectacular diving area
is at **Dwejra Point**, with deep
water and many caves and
arches. The most dramatic is the
115-foot (35m) tunnel which
opens from the Inland Sea to the
open sea.

Guests of the Ta'Cenc Hotel
may use **Mġarr-ix-Xini**: the
entrance to the water is from the
hotel's private beach.

On Comino, at the southwest tip,
is a thin strip of land called **Ras**

l-Irqieqa, where there is a sheer drop-off to 130 feet (40m). Shoals of sardine are among the delights to be seen on a dive here.

St Marija Caves are an interesting shallow location for a relaxing dive and endless possibilities for imaginative underwater photography. Snorkelling is fine in all the swimming areas, and just needs basic instruction. You can rent everything you need at any of the beach centres.

Fishing

You don't need a licence to go fishing in Malta, but you do need a friendly fisherman to take you out to sea. Try asking around Marsaxlokk Bay or Mġarr Harbour in Gozo.

Football

Probably Malta's best-loved sport. The season is between September and May, when league championships and other competitions are played. A major venue is the National Stadium at Ta'Qali; there is also a stadium at Gzira.

Golf

An 18-hole golf course and 18-hole mini golf corse are located at the Marsa Sports Club (see page 106). Some hotels have a mini golf facility as well.

Health Clubs

A number of the better hotels feature health and leisure clubs, among them the Holiday Inn Crowne Plaza in Sliema and the Jerma Palace in Marsaskala (see Accommodation, page 96). The Sports Connection, part of the Eden Beach Hotel in St

George's Bay, has a gym, indoor heated pool, sauna and whirlpool.

Horse Racing

Horse racing is high on the list of spectator sports, with Sunday meets at the Marsa racecourse between October and May. Most of the races – there are usually eight or nine – are for trotters.

Horse Riding

There are several riding schools within the vicinity of the Marsa race track and some hotels offer riding facilities. Centres include: Darmanin Riding School, 15 Stables Lane, Marsa (tel: 23 56 49); Josephine Riding School, Racecourse Street, Marso (no telephone); Golden Bay Hotel Riding School, Golden Bay (tel: 57 39 61); Mellieħa Holiday Centre Riding School, Mellieħa Bay (tel: 57 39 01); Sant Cassia Riding School, c/o Ta Cassia Restaurant, Qawra (tel: 47 14 35); and St Andrew's Riding Stable, St Andrew's (tel: 34 25 08).

Paragliding

Paragliding is available at Golden Sands, Mellieħa Bay, Golden Bay, Qawra, St George's Bay and St Julian's.

Squash

One of the best places for squash is the Marsa Sports Club, (see page 106) but several hotels do have their own courts.

Swimming

You are free to swim almost everywhere in Malta and there is sandy beach space at the following spots: Armier Bay (Bus 50), Balluta Bay (Bus 62), Għajn

Tuffieħa (among the best; Bus 47), Ghar Lapsi (Bus 94), Gnejna Bay (one of the best, but less easy to reach by bus), Golden Bay (highly recommended, Bus 47), Mellieħa Bay (also highly recommended; Bus 45/48), Mistra Bay, near St Paul's Bay (not readily reached by bus), Paradise Bay (well recommended; Bus 45) Pretty Bay (Bus 11), Ir-Ramla (Bus 48), St George's Bay (Bus 68), St Thomas Bay (not readily reached by bus; north of Marsaxlokk), White Tower Bay (also difficult to reach by bus; on the northeastern tip) and Xemxija Bay (Bus 43).

The rocky beach sites can be quite scenic – and at least a picnic lunch will stay free of sand! Some suggestions are: Anchor Bay (not very accessible; on the island's northwestern corner), Baħar ic-Caghaq (Bus 68), Buġibba (popular; Bus 49), Delimara (not on a bus route; on the southeastern point), Exiles (Bus 62), Font Ghadir (Bus 62), Marsaskala (recommended; Bus 19), Marsaxlokk (Bus 27), Peter's Pool (scenic, but not on a bus route; north of Delimara Point), Qawra (popular; Bus 49), Qui-s-Sana, near Sliema (Bus 62), St Paul's Bay (recommended; Bus 43), Salina (not on a bus route), and Wied iż-Żurrieq (Bus 38).

Gozo's rocky bathing places are Xlendi, where there is sand as well, the Inland Sea at Dwejra, Marsalforn and Qala. The best sandy beach is Ir-Ramla and, to a lesser extent, San Blas Bay, east of Ir-Ramla and not as accessible.

Tennis

The **Marsa Sports Club** (see page 106) has first class courts. Many hotels also have tennis courts and facilities for table tennis.

Waterskiing

Waterskiing is available at the larger hotels and beaches at St Paul's Bay, Mellieħa, Sliema, Salina Bay, St George's Bay and Golden Bay.

Windsurfing

Windsurfing (boardsailing) has become increasingly popular in Malta, to such an extent that there are two international competitions: the Sicily-Malta Windsurfing Race, which takes place in May, and the International Open Class Boardsailing Championships, which are held in September. Windsurfing for fun may be enjoyed in any of the sheltered northern bays. The **Ramla Bay Hotel** at Marfa (tel: 47 35 22) offers courses and hourly lessons, and will rent out boards. At Mellieħa Bay, the **Tunny Net** (tel: 47 43 38), the **Maxim Lido** (tel: 47 39 95), the **Seabank Water Sports Centre** (tel: 47 31 16) and the **Mellieħa Bay Hotel** (tel: 47 38 44) offer windsurfing lessons and boards. In St Julian's **Divewise Services** (tel: 33 64 41) is open all year round and offers training courses as well as rentals. The **Xemxija Hotel** at St Paul's Bay (tel: 47 34 54) has a German Surf School and facilities are also available at Golden Bay, the **Jerma Palace Hotel** at Marsaskala (tel: 82 32 22) and the **Sunny Coast Leisure and Fitness Centre** at Qawra Bay.

DIRECTORY

Contents

Arriving	Numbers	Public Transport
Camping	Health	Senior Citizens
Crime	Holidays	Student and Youth
Customs	Lost Property	Travel
Regulations	Media	Telegrams
Disabled	Money Matters	Telephone
Driving	Opening Times	Time
Electricity	Personal Safety	Tipping
Embassies and	Pharmacies	Toilets
Consulates	Places of Worship	Tourist Offices
Emergency	Police	Travel Agencies
Telephone	Post Office	

Arriving

Luqa International Airport (tel: 24 34 55; or 88 29 16/88 29 26 for reservations) is situated about 4 miles (6km) south of Valletta and takes a 15-minute drive. The airport is reasonably well serviced, with a restaurant, 24-hour currency exchange, car hire desks, information counter, post office and a small duty free shop. The best way to reach Valletta is by taxi, since the bus service into town is not very frequent. If you are travelling as part of a holiday package,

coach transport to your destination will probably be provided.

Air Malta flies from several European destinations, including Austria, Belgium Denmark, France, Germany, Greece, Italy and the UK. Its Malta office is at 285 Triq ir Repubblika, Valletta (tel: 22 12 07/23 68 16/22 07 66).

There is no airport on Gozo. Visitors from the UK, US,

On the runway at Luqa International Airport

Carriage awaits at Mdina Cathedral

Canada, New Zealand and Australia can travel to Malta on a standard passport; no visa is required for a stay under three months.

Camping
There are no campsites on any of the islands.

Crime
Malta is not ridden with crime and you are safe more or less anywhere. Do take the normal precautions against theft by leaving valuables in the hotel safe, not on the beach, and locking your car (see **Police**, page 120).

Customs Regulations
Every adult visitor is allowed to bring in 200 cigarettes (or 50 cigars or 250g of tobacco) duty free, plus one litre of spirits and one litre of wine. Personal effects and clothing which are for use on holiday are not subject to duty.

There is no restriction on how much foreign currency you bring in with you, but you are only entitled to import LM50 in local currency and export up to LM25 when you leave.

Disabled

Although some hotels have facilities for people with disabilities, Malta is not an ideal destination; for instance, many of the beaches are rocky and difficult for wheelchairs. Historic sites can be steep and often involve climbing steps. Places which might pose particular problems are Valletta, Għar Dalam, Mdina, Gozo Citadel and several individual churches and museums, which are reached via steps. The restaurant at Luqa Airport is also reached by steps, and buses have high platforms.

The **Paola Rehabilitation Centre** can arrange the hire of wheelchairs and other equipment: it is based at Corradino, Paola, Malta (tel: 23 75 18/22 22 21).

Driving

There is a wide choice of **car hire** in Malta, where all the major companies are represented. Cost of car hire varies according to company and duration, but it is one of the cheapest in Europe. Major companies will accept credit cards for payment (although some may ask for a cash deposit). The only document you need is an international driving licence, but the minimum age is usually 25.

Alpine: 33 73 61
Avis: 22 59 86
Gazan Holidays: 31 27 73
HIX Car Hire: 33 55 77
John's Garage (Europcar agent): 23 87 45
Merlin: 22 31 31
St Patrick's Rent-a-Car: 33 09 27
Sterling: 33 09 25
United Garage (Hertz agent): 31 46 30

Wembley Motors (also a mini cab service): 33 54 36

Chauffer-driven cars are available but very expensive. If you don't wish to drive yourself, strike a bargain with a taxi driver for a day's outing.

Fuel is readily available but costly. All service stations close on Sundays, so make sure you have sufficient fuel in the tank on a Saturday night if you're planning an excursion.

Rules of the road aren't always adhered to by the locals, but theoretically driving is on the left and speed limits are 25mph (40kph) in built-up areas and 34mph (55kph) on larger roads. Overtaking is on the right, and, at roundabouts, give right-of-way to cars already in the circuit.

Road conditions are not always perfect, and there are few stretches that can be likened to a motorway. For the most part, country roads are very narrow, with hairpin bends (so use the horn), often potholed and in need of repair, and if there has been rain, can get flooded. Parking is also a problem, especially in Valletta or in the vicinity of Mdina, both of which have large pedestrianised zones. There are no meters in Malta and you won't get clamped, but expect a fine if you park illegally.

Traffic police aren't normally too visible, but they do exist. If you break down in a hired car, call the company to send help. If you have an accident, call the police immediately: tel: 191, and don't move the vehicle until they get there. (Claims are not usually settled until the police make an on-the-spot report.)

DIRECTORY

Electricity
The standard current is 240 volts, 50 cycles.

Embassies and Consulates
Australia: High Commission, Airways House, Gaiety Lane, Sliema (tel: 33 82 01/5).
Canada: Canadian Consulate, 103 Triq l-Arcisqof (Archbishop Street), Valletta (tel: 23 31 22). The nearest embassy is in Rome (tel: (396) 844 1841).
New Zealand: the nearest embassy is in Rome (tel: (396) 440 2928).
UK: High Commission, 7 St Anne Street, Floriana (tel: 23 31 34/8).
US: Embassy, Development House, St Anne Street, Floriana (tel: 62 36 53).

Emergency Telephone Numbers
Police: 191
Ambulance: 196
Fire: 199
Doctor: 196

Health
Hygiene standards are high in Malta and you may not have any tummy problems, although high summer heat might affect you. Theoretically, the water is safe to drink in hotels and restaurants, but it may be best to buy bottled water. (Most mineral water comes from Italy, but the local brand is Farson's *San Michele*, which is slightly bubbly.)

Use your common sense when you sit out in the sun by making sure that your sun screen, cream or lotion is of a high enough factor. Also bring or buy some insect repellant: it's not that Malta is invaded with hordes of mosquitoes, but it does get its fair share.

Medical treatment in Malta is of a high standard. The UK has a reciprocal agreement with Malta to provide free health care: take the appropriate form (available from your local Department of Health and Social Security).

If you need a doctor urgently, ask your hotel (the better ones have a doctor on call) or dial 196. The hospital to call in Malta is St Luke's in Gwardamanga (tel: 24 12 51); in Gozo, call the Craig Hospital in Victoria (tel: 55 68 51).

International medicines are available over the counter or by prescription at most chemists, but if you are on drugs for medical purposes, make sure you have enough with you and/or a letter from your doctor. It is always wise to take out medical insurance, and in the case of visitors from the US, Canada, Australia and New Zealand, it is essential. Visitors from the UK, US, Canada, Australia and Europe do not need any vaccination or inoculation certificates.

Holidays
The main public holidays are as follows:
1 January: New Year's Day
10 February: Feast of St Paul's Shipwreck
19 March: Feast of St Joseph
31 March: Freedom Day
Easter: Good Friday (dates vary)
1 May: Workers' Day
7 June: *Sette Giugno* (sometimes celebrated)
29 June: Feast of St Peter and St Paul

15 August: Feast of the
Assumption
8 September: Victory Day
21 September: Independence
Day
8 December: Feast of the
Immaculate Conception
13 December: Republic Day
25 December: Christmas Day
Every town and village
celebrates the feast day of its
own patron saint.

Lost Property
Check carefully to make sure
you really have lost an item
before reporting it. Property
inadvertently left on a café
table, etc, is unlikely to be
stolen and may well be taken to
the nearest police station. If you
lose something valuable, call the
police (see **Police**, page 120).

Media
In main towns such as Valletta
you should be able to buy many
English-language daily papers
on the day of publication,
including the *International
Herald Tribune;* in Gozo, it may
be available the day after
publication.
The local English-language
daily paper is *The Times of
Malta*, and there are two
weeklies: *The Democrat* and
The Sunday Times. Look out,
too, for the tourist guide *What's
On*, which is printed fortnightly.
Radio Malta broadcasts daily in
English and Italian and BBC

The ferry approaching Sliema

DIRECTORY

Taking a dip in Senglea docks

World Service will come over clearly on short wave bands. Television features programmes in Maltese and English, including many American and British favourites. A number of hotels offer in-house TV and videos, or have bought into one of the international networks.

Money Matters

Currency is decimal. The Maltese lira is divided into 100 cents, and each cent is divided into 10 mils. Notes are available in denominations of LM20, LM10, LM5, LM2 and LM1. Coins come in denominations of 50, 25, 10, 5, 2 and 1 cents and 5, 3 and 2 mils. The Central Bank of Malta in Valletta issues the official rate of exchange daily.

Money may be exchanged at the airport, at most banks and hotels.

Banks: the leading commercial bank is the Bank of Valletta, whose main office is at 45 Triq ir Repubblika (tel: 22 24 31). There are other Valletta offices at Misrah San Gorg (St George's Square), Customs House and Pjazza San Gwann (St John's Square). In Sliema, there are branches at The Strand and High Street; in Rabat at Saqqajja Square. There are 20 other branches in Malta and Gozo, including Luqa Airport. The Mid-Med Bank, whose main office is 32-34 Triq il-Merkanti (Merchants Street), Valletta (tel:

24 52 81), also has other Valletta branches at 233 Triq ir Repubblika (Republic Street) and 17 Lascaris Wharf. In Sliema there's a branch on High Street and at 112 Manwel Dimech Street; in Rabat at Saqqajja Square; in St Julian's at St George's Road and in St Paul's Bay at 551 St Paul Street. There are 27 other branches in Malta and Gozo. The Lombard Bank is located on Triq ir Repubblika in Valletta (tel: 62 06 32).

Banking hours are usually 08.00-12.00 hrs Monday to Friday, 08.00-11.30 hrs on Saturday (in summer); and 08.30-12.30 hrs Monday to Friday, 08.30-12.00hrs on Saturday (in winter). However, foreign exchange facilities are available after normal hours at many branches of the Bank of Valletta and Mid-Med Bank: 16.00-19.00 hrs in summer and 15.00-18.00 hrs in winter. Luqa Airport's exchange facility is open 24 hours. There is also an exchange bureau at 58 Triq il-Merkanti, Valletta and one at 6 Ross Street, Paceville, open daily (not Sunday) 09.00-12.30 hrs and 15.00-18.00 hrs. All the major credit cards are widely used and accepted at hotels, restaurants and shops.

Opening Times

Restaurant, bar and café opening hours vary, but can extend from 09.00 to 01.00 hrs. Alcoholic beverages may be bought at any hour. Shops are generally open daily (not Sunday) 09.00-19.00 hrs but will close for a two- or three-hour lunch. The open-air market on Triq il-Merkanti, Valletta, operates mornings only, Monday to Saturday. On Sundays, a much larger morning market takes place at St James's Ditch, just outside Valletta. General office hours are 08.30 or 09.00-13.00 or 13.30 hrs; and 14.30-17.30 or 18.00 hrs, Monday to Friday.

Most museums are open 07.45-14.00 hrs in summer (16 June to 30 September) and 08.15-17.00 hrs Monday to Saturday, and to 16.00 hrs on Sunday, in winter (1 October to 15 June). They all close on public holidays. (Since almost all museums are state-run, opening hours are standard. However, St John's Co-Cathedral Museum in Valletta is private, and opens Monday to Saturday 09.00-13.00 hrs and 15.00-17.30 hrs; so is the Mdina Cathedral Museum in Mdina, which opens Monday to Saturday, 09.30-13.00 hrs and 14.00-17.30 hrs.)

Fuel stations are open Monday to Saturday, 07.00-18.00 hrs (some fuel stations remain open until 19.00 hrs during the summer).

Personal Safety

You have little to fear in Malta, since the crime rate is very low, and the Maltese are generally honest and courteous. Women may find that they are wolf-whistled, but there is unlikely to be any persistent harassment.

Pharmacies

In Malta a pharmacy is usually known as a chemist, and you will find one in every town and village. Most are adequately stocked with well-known

DIRECTORY

medicines and toiletries. The usual opening hours are 08.30-13.00 and 15.00-19.00 hrs, Monday to Saturday. On Sundays, one chemist per district will be open: check with your hotel or the local Sunday paper. There are branches of Boots the Chemist in Valletta and Sliema, and items such as nappies, baby foods and tampons are readily available.

Places of Worship

Malta is a Catholic country, and almost all the churches are of that denomination.

There are countless churches on the islands, to be found in every town and village. Most services are in Maltese, but masses are held in English on Sundays at the following: St Max Kolbe Church, Buġibba; Our Lady's Shrine, Mellieħa; St Dominic's Church, Rabat; Convent of the Sacred Heart, St Julian's; Parish Church of Our Lady of Sorrows, St Paul's Bay; St Patrick's Church, Sliema; St John of the Cross Church, Ta'Xbiex; Our Lady of Victories Church and St Barbara's, both in Valletta; and St Joseph the Worker Church, Xemxija. Other denominational churches are Anglican, Church of Scotland and Greek Orthodox.

Police

Police headquarters are in Floriana. For general enquiries tel: 22 40 01; for traffic accidents tel: 191. In Gozo, the main police station is on Triq ir-Repubblika in Victoria, tel: 55 64 30 (to be used for all enquiries).

Post Office

The main post offices are:

General Post Office, Triq il-Merkanti, Valletta; 21 Wilgar Street, Paceville, St Julian's; Islets Promenade, Buġibba; and Manwel Dimech Street, Sliema. In Gozo branches are at 129 Triq ir-Repubblika, Victoria and St Anthony Street, Mġarr. The Valletta office is open 07.30-18.00 hrs, Monday to Saturday in summer and 08.00-18.30 hrs in winter (08.00-12.00 hrs on Sunday). Branch offices open 07.30-12.45 hrs Monday to Saturday all year round.

The Victoria office is open 08.00-12.30 hrs Monday to Friday, to 11.00 hrs on Saturday in summer; and 08.00-12.30 hrs and 13.15-16.00 hrs Monday to Friday, 08.00-11.00 hrs on Saturday in winter.

The postal service is efficient and stamps may be bought at most hotels and some tobacconists.

Public Transport

Getting around by public transport is very easy on Malta, but less so on Gozo.

Bus Most of Malta's towns and villages are connected to Valletta by local bus services. Usually, they depart from and return to City Gate, the main terminus. The destination drop-off point is almost always in the central square by the parish church. Buses (coloured green) are numbered but not marked with their destination: any enquiries may be made at the Despatcher's Kiosk at City Gate (tel: 22 40 01).

The most regular Gozo service meets the ferry at Mġarr, with a drop-off point in Victoria and, in

Fishermen prepare for the catch

summer, to Marsalforn and Xlendi. Villages on this island do run their own buses, which stop at Victoria's Main Gate Street terminus, but timings are rather unreliable.

Ferry Both Gozo and Comino are reached by ferry. Services from Malta to Gozo depart either from Sa Maison pier at Pieta Creek (a one-hour, 15-minute trip) or from Ċirkewwa (a 20-minute ride). Services are frequent and, in summer, continue through the night, but bad winter weather may upset the schedules. Ferry services to Comino are

also available from both Malta and Gozo.

Helicopter A service between Malta and Gozo was introduced in 1990 as the first alternative to the traditional ferry. The 13-seater helicopters operate from Luqa Airport, during the summer only. The price is not a great deal more than travel by boat.

Taxis You can hail taxis in the street if they have white licence plates and red numbers; those with red licence plates and black numbers are hired by phone.

DIRECTORY

Valletta bus station

All taxis are metered, although you can negotiate with the driver for a day's outing. The large hotels have taxi ranks or will call one for you. You will find taxi stands are located at Luqa Airport, City Gate and Palace Square, Valletta, and also on the promenade at Sliema. (Wembley Motors offer a 24-hour mini cab service, tel: 33 54 36).

In Gozo, you will find taxis at Mġarr Harbour and in Pjazza Indipendenza (It-Tokk Square), Victoria.

Horse-drawn cabs, called *karozzin*, are popular with tourists, but agree on a fare before you get in. You will find them at City Gate, Misrah l-Assedju l-Kbir (Great Siege Square) and the Customs House in Valletta; on the promenade at Sliema; and in Bastion Square at Mdina.

Senior Citizens

Malta tends to be a popular holiday destination for senior citizens and several long-stay winter packages are available. There are no specific discounts available from the Maltese government, but transport and admission fees are generally inexpensive. Saga has offices in the UK and the US:

Saga Holidays Ltd, Saga Building, Middelburg Square, Folkestone, Kent CT20 1AZ (tel: 0303 857000);

Saga International, 120 Boylton Street, Boston, Massachusetts 02116 (tel: 617 451 6808).

Student and Youth Travel

The only real concessions for young people are on air travel to Malta; discounts are given on some museum admission prices. Contact the **Youth Travel Circle**, Rabat (tel: 23 38 93).

Telegrams

Telemalta offers a 24-hour service at St George's Road, St Julian's (tel: 33 40 20) and during office hours at the Valletta

branch in Triq Nofs-in-Nhar (South Street). A telex service is available between 07.00 and 19.00 hrs at the St Julian's office and at Luqa Airport.
To send a cable from Gozo, tel: 83 40 42.

Telephone

Malta's public telephone boxes are painted blue. Telephone directory information is listed in Maltese and English. For local enquiries, dial 190.
Nowadays, you can direct-dial many countries. The overseas access code is 00, and international country codes are as follows:
Ireland 00353
Australia 0061
New Zealand 0064
UK 0044
US and Canada 001
Omit the initial zero of the destination area code.
To reach the overseas operator, dial 194. The telephone operator on Gozo is 55 69 99.
To call Malta from abroad, use the following codes before the main number:
from **Australia** 0011 356
from **Ireland** 16 356
from **New Zealand** 00 356
from **UK** 010 356
from **US and Canada** 011 356

Time

Maltese time is one hour ahead of GMT; six hours ahead of New York; four and a half to 10 hours ahead of Canada; nine hours ahead of San Francisco; seven hours ahead of New Orleans; 11 hours behind New Zealand; eight and a half hours behind Southern Australia and seven hours behind Western Australia.

Tipping

Restaurants may or may not include a service charge, but even if they do, leave a little loose change. If they don't, a 10-15 per cent tip is average. A 10 per cent government levy has, however, now been introduced.

Toilets

Public toilets are scarce and are not that recommendable. Most cafés and bars do have clean toilets which you can use.

Tourist Offices

The **National Tourism Organisation of Malta** is based at 280 Triq ir Repubblika, Valletta (tel: 22 44 44). There is a UK office at Suite 300, Mappin House, 4 Winsley Street, London W1N 7AR (tel: (071) 323 0506). Information on Malta is available in Ireland from: Sean Carberry Associates, 22 Ely Place, Dublin 2 (tel: (1) 611 044); and in the US from the Permanent Mission of Malta to the United Nations, 249 East 35th Street, New York, NY10016 (tel: (212) 725 2345/9). There is a tourist information office in Valletta at City Gate Arcade (open Monday to Saturday, 08.30-12.30 hrs and 13.15-18.00 hrs; on public holidays 08.30-13.00 hrs and 15.00-18.00 hrs; on Sundays 08.30-13.00 hrs). Other information centres can be found on Bisazza Street, Sliema; Main Street, St Julian's; Buġibba and at Mġarr Harbour, Gozo. The main Gozo Tourist Office is at Pjazza Indipendenzia, Victoria. Tourists with any complaints should call 60 56 15; outside office hours, a message can be left on the answering machine.

Travel Agencies

Travel agencies are most numerous in Valletta, Sliema and St Paul's Bay. Details of sightseeing tours are generally available at your hotel; it is worth asking at the desk for information, or simply keeping an eye open for offices in the major resorts and centres.

A peaceful side street on the island of Gozo

Captain Morgan Cruises, 77 The Strand, Sliema (tel: 33 19 61/33 65 76) offer cruises from The Strand to Comino, round Malta and round the harbour, and there are also day trips available from Malta to Gozo.

LANGUAGE

The Maltese language is basically semitic, derived from Phoenician and influenced by the Arabs: over the years it has also absorbed French, Italian and English words and phrases. The end result is a unique and complex language, Il-Malti, which existed only as a spoken language until a written form was eventually introduced in the 20th century.

Pronunciation

The key points to remember for pronunciation are the following:
An **x** is pronounced as *sh*, so that Xlendi, for instance, is pronounced *Shlendi*.
The **j** is soft, so that Lija is pronounced *Liya*.
An accented **ġ** is as the *g* in *George*. Without an accent, the **g** is hard.
ċ is pronounced *ch*, as in *church*; Kerċem is pronounced *Kerchem*.
A **għ** is generally silent, except when it is at the end of a word or followed by an *i* or *u*.
An **h** is usually silent; an **ħ** is aspirated.
A **q** has a slight sound like a glottal stop or *kh*.
aj sounds like *igh* in *high*, and **ej** like *ay* in *say*.
z (without an accent) is pronounced *ts;* with an accent (**ż**) it is pronounced *z* as in *zebra*.

The Alphabet

There are 29 letters in the Maltese alphabet (24 of which are consonants);
a, b, ċ, d, e, f, ġ, g, għ, h, ħ, i, j, k, l, m, n, o, p, q, r, s, t, u, v, w, x, z, ż.

Basic Phrases

Bonju *(bonjoo)* good morning
Bonswa good evening
Iva *(eeva)* yes
Le *(leh)* no
Jekk joghgbok *(yeck yojbok)* please
Grazzi (pronounced as Italian) thank you
Skuzi (pronounced as Italian) excuse me
Fejn hu *(fayn noo)* where is
Kemm *(kehm)* how much

Numbers

Wiehed *(weehehd)* one
Tnejn *(tnayn)* two
Tlieta *(tleeta)* three
Erbgħa *(ehrba)* four
Hamsa *(humsar)* five
Sitta *(sittar)* six
Sebgħa *(sehbah)* seven
Tmienja *(tmee-ehnyah)* eight
Disgħa *(disah)* nine
Għaxra *(ashrah)* ten

Putting the world to rights

INDEX

Page numbers in italics
refer to illustrations.

Abbatija tad Dejr
    Roman Catacombs
    63-4
accommodation 94-8,
    103
airports and air
    services 113-4
Archaeological
    Museum 75
Argotti Botanical
    Gardens 40
Attard 55
Auberges 26-8, 27

Balluta 49
Balzan 55
banks 118-19
Bastions 29-30
Biblioteca 30
bird migration 85-6
birdlife 82, 84, 85-6
Birkirkara 45
Birżebbuġa 65, 65
Blue Grotto 68, 69
Blue Lagoon 80
Borġ in-Nadur 8, 65
budget tips 103
Buġibba 53
buses 103, 120-1
Buskett Gardens 64,
    82

Calypso's Cave 79
camping 114
car hire 115
Casa Inguanez 61
Casa Leoni 46
Cathedral (Mdina)
    61-2, 114
Cathedral (Valletta) 38,
    39
Cathedral (Victoria) 75
Cathedral Museum
    (Mdina) 62
Cathedral Museum
    (Victoria) 75
Chadwick Lakes 84
Chapel of the
    Annunciation 78
chemists 119-20
children's
    entertainment 102

Church of the
    Immaculate
    Conception 76
Church of Our Lady of
    Victory 44
Church of St Gregory
    51
Church of St John the
    Baptist 80
Church of St Lawrence
    42
church services 120
Chapham Junction 64
climate 99-100
Collegiate Church of St
    Helen 45
Comino 80, 80
Cominotto 80
Cospicua 44
Cotonera Lines 44
craft centres 94
currency 118
customs regulations
    114

Delimara 82
Delimara Point 67
Dingli 59, 59
disabled travellers 115
dress 100
driving 115
duty-free allowances
    114
Dwejra 75-6
Dwejra Point 76

embassies and
    consulates 116
emergencies 116
entry regulations 113-4

ferries 121
festivals and events
    104-6
Filfla 59, 82
Floriana 40, 92
Fontana 76, 76
food and drink 87-91
Fort Chambray 77
Fort Ricasoli 31
Fort St Angelo 31, 43
Fort St Elmo 30
Fort Tigné 49

Gesù 30

Ġgantija temples 8, 79,
    79
Ghadira 85
Għajn Rasul 53
Għajn Tuffieħa 6, 52
Għar Dalam 7-8, 65
Għar il-kbin 83
Għar Lapsi 82
Għarb 76
Għargħur 45
Għaxaq 66
gifts and souvenirs
    92-4
Gozo 70-80, 72, 124
    map 70-1
Gozo Heritage 77
Grand Harbour 31
Grotto of St Paul 63
Grotto of San Martin 53
Gudja 66
guest houses 97
Gwarena Tower 69
Gzira 45

Ħaġar Qim 7, 66
Ħal Millieri 69
Ħal Saflieni Hypogeum
    8, 47-9
Ħamrun 45-6
handicrafts 92, 92-4
Hastings Gardens 29
health matters 116
history of Malta 5, 7-23
horse-drawn cabs 114,
    122
hotels 94-7

Il-Ġebla tal-Ġeneral
    75-6
Il-Gzejjer 53
Il-Kastell 74, 74-5
Il-Maqluba 69
Il-Nuffara 9
Inland Sea 76
Inquisitor's Summer
    Palace 57-8
Ir-Ramla 76, 77
Isola Point 44

John F Kennedy
    Memorial Olive
    Grove 54

Kalafrana 65
Kalkara 46

Kercem 78
Kirkop 66
Knights of St John
14-20, *15*
Knights' Wash House
78

La Vittoria 34
language 125
Lija 55
local etiquette 100-1
local hygiene 116, 123
local time 123
lost property 117
Lower Barracca
Gardens 30
Luqa 46

Madalena Chapel 59
Maglio Gardens 40
Malta Government
Craft Centre 94
Maltese Ornithological
Society 86
Manderaggio 29
Manoel Island 30, 45
Manoel Theatre 34
maps
Gozo 70-1
Malta 4, 12-13
Mdina 60
Rabat 62
Valletta 32-3
Valletta environs 41
Victoria 73
maquis and *garigue*
vegetation 82-3
Margherita Lines 44
markets 94
Marsa Creek 31
Marsalforn 77, 92
Marsamxett Harbour
46
Marsaskala 46
Marsaxlokk 66-7, *67*,
101
Mdina 60-2, *61*, *81*
map 60
medical insurance 116
medical treatment 116
Mediterranean
Conference Centre
102
Mellieħa Bay 52, *52*,
108

Mġarr 53, 76-7
Mġarr-ix-Xini 78, 86
Mistra Bay 53
Mnajdra 8, 68
money 118-19
Mosta 55-6, *56*
Mqabba 69
Msida 46
Mtahleb 86

Nadur 78
National Museum of
Archaeology 28
National Museum of
Fine Arts 34
Natural History
Museum 61
Naxxar 57, *57*, *58*
Naxxar Ridge 45
newspapers 117-18
nightlife and
entertainment 98-9
Ninu's Cave 79

opening times 119

Palace of the Grand
Masters 35, *35*, *36*,
37
Palazzo Bondi 75
Palazzo Falzon 62
Palazzo del Sant'Uffizio
42-3
Palazzo Santa Sophia
62
Paola *47*, 47-9
personal safety 114,
119
Pinto Battery 65
places of worship 120
police 120
Porte des Bombes 40
post offices 120
prehistoric sites 7-10
public holidays 116-17
public transport 120-2
Pwales Valley 54

Qala 78
Qawra 53
Qbajjar 77
Qormi 49
Qrendi 69

Rabat *10*, *11*, 63-4, *64*

map 62
radio and television
118
Ras ir-Raħeb 82
restaurants 89-91, 103
Roman Villa and
Museum 63
Royal Naval Hospital 46
Rundle Gardens 73

Sacra Infirmeria 37
St Andrew's 49
St Augustine's Church
63
St Catherine Tat-Torba
69
St Catherine's Church
34
St George 75
St George's Bay 49
St John's Co-Cathedral
38, *39*
St Julian's *48*, 49
St Julian's Tower 49
St Mary 'Ta Bir Miftuħ'
66
St Mary's Church 56, *56*
St Paul and St Agatha
Catacombs 63
St Paul's Bay 53-4, *54*
St Paul's Church 63
St Paul's Shipwreck *39*
St Thomas Tower 46
Salina Bay 54, 84-5
San Anton Palace and
Gardens 55
San Pawl Milqi 54
San Pawl Tat-Targa 57
Sanctuary of the
Immaculate
Conception 78
Sannat 78
Santa Barbara 40
Santa Venera 46
Senglea 31, 43-4, *44*,
118
senior citizens 122
shopping 92-4
Siġġiewi 57-8
Skorba 8, 53
Sliema 49, 92, *117*
Spinola 49
sport and leisure
activities 106-12, *108*,
109, *110*

INDEX/ACKNOWLEDGEMENTS

spring flowers 83, *83*
student and youth travel 122

Ta 'Cenc 78, 82
Ta 'Dbiergi Crafts Village 94
Ta 'Hagrat 53
Tal-Lunzjata Chapel and Catacombs 54
Tal-Lunzjata Valley 78
Tal-Mentna Catacombs 69
Tal-Mirakli Church 55
Tal 'Qrogg 46
Ta 'Pinu Basilica 78
Ta 'Qali 64
Ta 'Qali Craft Centre 94
Tarxien 8, *9*, 50, *50*
Tas-Silg 67
taxis 121-2
telegrams 122-3
telephones 123
The Three Cities 42-4
Tieqa Zerqa 76
tipping 123

toilets 123
Torre dello Standardo 61
tourist apartments 97-8
tourist offices 123
traditional dishes 87-9
travel agencies 124

Upper Barracca Gardens 40

Valletta *16*, *17*, 18, 19, *19*, *24*, 25-40, *28-9*, *31*, 85, *91*, 92, *93*, *122*
    map 32-3
Verdala Palace 64
Victoria Lines 45
Victoria (Rabat) 73-5, 92
    map 73
Vilhena Palace 61
Vittoriosa 42, *43*
voltage 116

War Museum 30
Wardija Heights 53

Wied Girgenti Valley 57
Wied il-Luq 82, 86
Wied Znuber 86
Wignacourt Tower 53
wildlife and countryside 81-6
words and phrases 125

Xaghra 79
Xaghra Plateau 79
Xarolla Windmill 69
Xemxija 82
Xerri's Grotto 79
Xewkija 80
Xlendi 80, 86, 92
Xwieni 77

youth hostels 103

Żabbar 51, *51*
Żebbuġ 8, 58
Żejtun 51
Żurrieq 69

The Automobile Association would like to thank the following photographers, libraries and associations for their assistance in the preparation of this book.

PHILIP ENTICKNAP took all the photographs in this book (© AA Photo Library) except:

J ALLAN CASH PHOTO LIBRARY 47 Hypogeum Burial Site, 57/8 Naxxar Church

INTERNATIONAL PHOTOBANK Cover Marsaxlokk

MALTA NATIONAL TOURIST OFFICE 23 Independence

MARY EVANS PICTURE LIBRARY 15 Order of St John of Jerusalem, 16 Old Streets, Valletta, 20/1 French capture Malta

NATURE PHOTOGRAPHERS LTD 83 Rock Roses (B Burbidge), 84 Death's Head Hawk Moth Caterpillar (P R Sterry)

ROYAL AIR FORCE MUSEUM 22 Gladiator Aircraft

Philip Enticknap would also like to thank:

Malta National Tourist Office, London; Connie Grech, National Tourism Organisation, Malta; Air Malta, London and Luqa, Malta; Alpine Rent-a-Car, Malta; Les Lapins Hotel, Msida, Malta; Peter Darmanin, San Giuliano Restaurant, St Julians, Malta; Giannini Restaurant, Valletta; Manoel Theatre, Valletta; Malta Hilton; Dragonara Palace Casino; Eden Palladium; Styx 11 Discothèque; Dr AP Demajo; Mike Upton and Maltaque Diving School; Mr and Mrs JP de Bono, Casa Castelletti, Mdina; Museums Department, Malta; Mario the guide and Paul Curmi Dancers